w. e. lyons is professor of political science at the University of Kentucky. He is the author of *One Man–One Vote in Canada* and of numerous articles on consolidation and related topics.

The Politics of City-County Merger

The Politics of City-County Merger

The Lexington-Fayette County Experience

W. E. Lyons

The University Press of Kentucky

ISBN: 0-8131-1363-6

Library of Congress Catalog Card Number: 77-73706

Copyright © 1977 by The University Press of Kentucky

A statewide cooperative scholarly publishing agency
serving Berea College, Centre College of Kentucky,
Eastern Kentucky University, The Filson Club,
Georgetown College, Kentucky Historical Society,
Kentucky State University, Morehead State University,
Murray State University, Northern Kentucky University,
Transylvania University, University of Kentucky,
University of Louisville, and Western Kentucky University.

Editorial and Sales Offices: Lexington, Kentucky 40506

Contents

Tables and Figures

Preface

〜〜〜〜〜〜〜〜〜〜〜〜〜〜〜〜〜〜〜〜〜〜〜〜〜〜〜〜〜〜〜

THE POLITICS OF CITY-COUNTY MERGER is a study of the initiation, development, and eventual adoption of a proposal to consolidate the governments of the city of Lexington and Fayette County, Kentucky. It is also a study of how the Lexington experience squares with consolidation efforts in other communities since World War II.

It must be noted at the outset, however, that much of what follows is based on information I gathered while serving as a direct participant in the initiation and development of the Lexington merger proposal and as a consultant-participant during the campaign to secure voter approval of that proposal. I was a member of the small group of citizens who initiated and conducted the petition drive to get the city and county governments to establish a merger commission to develop a "comprehensive plan" or charter under the provisions of the state enabling statute. I was subsequently appointed to the merger commission and elected its chairman. Following the completion of the charter, I served as a consultant to a committee that was formed to conduct the referendum campaign, and I was an active spokesman for the proposed charter throughout the campaign.

Although this afforded me an opportunity to observe firsthand many of the nuances of the consolidation process, there should be no misunderstanding about where I stood on the question of merging city and county governments in Lexington. I hope that my training and experience as a political scientist specializing in the study of urban government and politics provides a reasonable counterbalance to the passion that goes with being an advocate for a particular point of view.

I wish to thank several people for their support and encouragement during both the merger process in Lexington and the writing of this study. I would like to offer special thanks to former Fayette County Judge Robert Stephens, who is currently the attorney general of Kentucky, for supporting merger from the outset and remaining a true friend of merger even after the charter commission decided to eliminate the executive and administrative powers that traditionally belonged to the office of county judge in Fayette County. Similarly, I wish to express my deepest gratitude to H. Foster Pettit, who became mayor of the city of Lexington at a very crucial point in the local city-county consolidation process. Without his cooperation as mayor, this volume on the success of the Lexington merger effort might not have been possible.

A special note of gratitude is also extended to the members of the Lexington-Fayette County Merger Commission for their tacit willingness to allow the author to retain the records and tape recordings of the proceedings of the commission and its various committees throughout the writing of this study. I also wish to thank various members of the commission for their cooperation in trying to clarify for me the meaning and substance of their remarks not clearly evident from either the tapes or written records of their deliberations.

Finally, I would like to express my gratitude to Penrose Ecton, Steve Driesler, and Dianne Smith who kept the author fully informed about the details surrounding the campaign phase of the Lexington merger effort. As leaders of the promerger campaign organization called the Committee to Insure Good Government, they were invaluable to the completion of this study. Penrose Ecton, who officially headed this group, passed away shortly after the Lexington merger charter was adopted. I would, therefore, like to dedicate this study to him—a true gentleman and ardent supporter of city-county consolidation in the Lexington area.

I

〰〰〰〰〰〰〰〰〰〰〰〰〰〰〰〰〰〰〰〰〰〰〰〰〰〰〰〰〰〰

Introduction

ON NOVEMBER 7, 1972, the voters of Lexington and Fayette County, Kentucky, decided by a rather substantial margin to consolidate their city and county governments into a single, unified, "urban county government."[1] From a strictly local perspective, the implications of this decision were of profound historical and political import. But there were more than local considerations at stake as the voters of this community responded to the merger question. They were participating in one of the most widely discussed "reform" movements in the history of the United States. Whatever their individual choices on the matter, the voters of Lexington and Fayette County were helping to write another chapter in the long and often contentious history of city-county consolidation.

Although much has been written on the subject, those interested in studying city-county consolidation have encountered several major difficulties. One problem has been that, while many communities have discussed the idea, relatively few have ever reached the point of making a final, authoritative decision on the matter. Furthermore, the opportunities we have had to examine the total consolidation process have been spread over several decades and have occurred in widely scattered places.

Given these problems, it is not surprising that much of the existing literature on the subject consists of little more than narrative accounts of the consolidation process in particular communities. Case studies of this type are always useful, but they rarely contribute much toward the development of a more systematic body of knowledge about the city-county consolidation process in general.

The problems associated with the study of city-county consolidation have also affected researchers interested in developing a more systematic, comparative approach to the subject. The difficulty of studying consolidation efforts in widely scattered places and times has led most researchers to focus on the stage in the total process that is most amenable to systematic analysis—voter reactions to consolidation proposals based on available aggregate data. Official election returns are readily available for consolidation referenda, and there is little difficulty in obtaining information about the social and economic traits of people living in various communities from the United States Census.

If one is content with trying to explain voter reactions to consolidation proposals on the basis of census information about large clusters of voters, this is a perfectly respectable way to proceed. But it limits the applicability of the research findings to a single step in the total process. Furthermore, it means trying to study what amounts to an individual act—voter-choice—on the basis of aggregate data.

Some efforts have been made to gather survey data about the attitudes and behavior of individual voters confronting consolidation choices. However, public opinion surveys are expensive. And when the opportunities to do this type of research occur over long periods of time and in scattered places, the odds are rather high that the findings will have been gathered by different researchers, using quite different methods and measures.[2] Thus, the advantages of this type of research are often canceled out by the lack of comparability between findings concerning the attitudes and behavior of voters in different consolidation settings. In the end, one is confronted with the choice between findings about voter behavior based on data concerning large aggregates of voters in a number of communities, and those based on survey studies of individual voter reactions in only one or two communities.

Neither option, of course, can fill the gaps in our understanding of the steps leading to the point at which the voters render a final, authoritative decision on a consolidation proposal. Unfortunately, the problem of studying these aspects of the consolidation process is compounded by a number of other difficulties. Relatively few people are involved in the initiation and development of consolidation proposals prior to election day. Little information, aggregate or otherwise, is readily available about these people, and the public record of their activities, values, and perceptions is generally very sparse. The cost of researching these questions is very high, and there is always the question of whether outside investigators can ever get at the essential facts needed to understand the complex and often contentious steps involved in the total consolidation process.

A number of things can be done, however, to improve our understanding of city-county consolidation attempts at the community level. One approach is to develop the traditional case study technique into a more meaningful instrument of inquiry. This is not to suggest that there is no further need for purely descriptive materials. Description is the first step toward understanding, and clearly there are many facets of city-county consolidation that have yet to be described in sufficient detail. But a more adequate handling of the case study technique may alleviate some of the problems of time, resources, and accessibility alluded to above.

It is the purpose of this study to examine the process of city-county consolidation by casting the events surrounding this process in Lexington and Fayette County, Kentucky, against the known dimensions of similar events in other communities. Obviously the quality of the generalizations that can be made will vary depending on the range and quality of the information available about various facets of the total process in other communities. Where information about other communities is missing or inadequate, efforts will be made to describe the situation in Lexington and Fayette County in sufficiently broad terms to allow future comparisons.

This is a study of city-county consolidation as it was initiated, developed, and eventually accepted by almost 70 percent of the voters in one of the relatively few communities to go through this process during the past several decades. It is hoped that it will illuminate and extend our understanding of the city-county consolidation process generally, while at the same time providing some insight into those aspects of the total process that have remained unexamined or only partially examined for many years.

2

The Consolidation Movement

THE HISTORY of city-county consolidation in the United States can be divided into two phases. The first phase began with the consolidation of New Orleans-Orleans County in 1805 and extended into the early decades of the twentieth century. During that period, consolidations were accomplished in such places as Boston, New York, Philadelphia, and San Francisco.

After a lull during the crisis years of the Great Depression and World War II, the consolidation movement was revived, but with a major change. Whereas all previous consolidations had been accomplished by state legislative action, after World War II voter approval was generally required before such a proposal could be implemented.[1] Several factors contributed to this change, including the success of civic reformers in securing the adoption of initiative, referendum, and home rule in many states during the 1920s and 1930s. Whatever the reasons, the only city-county consolidations attempted or accomplished strictly by state legislative action since World War II have been those in Indianapolis-Marion County, Indiana, in 1969 and Las Vegas-Clark County, Nevada, in 1975.[2] All others have required the approval of local voters.

Although the ground rules had changed, the basic arguments on behalf of consolidation remained the same. The major problem confronting most urban areas, according to the civic reformers, continued to be defined in terms of too many governments trying to serve what were viewed as essentially single socioeconomic units. Furthermore, the solution to this problem continued to be framed in terms of eradicating the "maze of local governments" found in most urban areas.³ A number of methods for accomplishing this task have been endorsed from time to time, including massive annexation and metropolitan federation. But for the most part, civic reformers have continued to reserve a special place in their hearts for the idea of consolidation as the most logical and comprehensive way to accomplish the kind of wholesale restructuring of urban governments which was felt to be required.⁴

The term city-county consolidation has been defined in a variety of ways, but the following definition contains the essential conditions that must be met before the term can be applied: "[Consolidation] involves the unification or merger of the governments of one or more cities with the government of the surrounding territory."⁵

This differs legally and substantively from annexation. Under an annexation proposal, one unit of local government, usually an incorporated municipality, extends its jurisdictional boundaries to include portions of the territorial area of another unit of government. Generally the area annexed is unincorporated territory, but the concept itself does not preclude the possibility of one incorporated area annexing territory from another.

Carried to its logical conclusion, the annexation process could result in an incorporated municipality extending its jurisdictional authority over an entire county. However, with the possible exception of such states as Virginia, where a legal separation is maintained between city and county jurisdictional territory, the extension of a city boundary to the county line through annexation generally results in nothing more than two units of general-purpose government sharing authority over the same geographical area. Thus, even the most ambitious program of annexation rarely results in the total unification of governmental units. And in many respects, it compounds the problem of overlapping responsibility that is so abhorrent to many civic reformers.

Metropolitan federation, on the other hand, divides jurisdictional authority between two levels of local government from the outset. The general pattern has been to retain all existing units of local government to perform certain specified functions, while creating a new, area-wide layer of government to perform other designated functions. The Canadians, who implemented the well-known federation in Toronto in 1953, have aptly described this alternative as a two-tiered system of metropolitan government.[6]

The extent to which the federation idea can be squared with the goals and assumptions of many civic reformers hinges on the number and type of functions assigned to the area-wide, metrogovernment authority. If these functions are extremely limited, federation becomes little more than another "special district." Placing a wide variety of powers and functions in the hands of the area-wide level of government can conceivably satisfy the basic goals of the reformers. However, the limited experience with the metropolitan federation idea in North America, including the initial Toronto Plan, has drawn criticism from some civic reformers for leaving too many area-wide functions with the lower tier of government.

Given these concerns, it is easy to understand why many civic reformers have viewed both massive annexation and metropolitan federation as preferable to creating more unifunctional special districts or more "ad hoc" interjurisdictional agreements to help solve the problems created by the maze of local governments found in most urban areas. However, these same concerns also help to explain why many civic reformers find the idea of consolidation to be both conceptually and operationally more in tune with their goal of creating a single, area-wide system of government to serve our burgeoning urban areas.

In some respects, the efforts of those who have pressed forward with consolidation have been well rewarded. The idea has been widely discussed for decades in national, state, and local forums. Numerous commissions have been formed to study the idea, and scores of consolidation proposals have been written. Several consolidated governments, particularly those in Nashville-Davidson County, Tennessee, and Jacksonville-Duval County, Florida, have received considerable national publicity and acclaim.

On the other hand, since World War II only forty different communities have managed to travel the long and difficult road between initiating discussions of the idea and presenting a formal consolidation plan to the voters. This is not a very impressive record given the number of urban communities in the United States with the problem of overlapping governments. Nor is it a very impressive record given the number of communities where the need for consolidation has been discussed.

But what about those instances in which city-county consolidation proposals actually reached the ballot? What does the won-lost record look like once a community has succeeded in developing an actual consolidation proposal to be submitted to the voters?

Clearly the won-lost record at this stage in the process has not been very encouraging to the civic reformers (see Table 1). A total of fifty-six consolidation referenda were conducted in forty communities between 1947 and 1976. Only thirteen of these consolidation proposals have been approved by local voters. Moreover, city-county consolidation has been placed before the voters of eight communities on the list on more than one occasion. Of these, only two have ultimately adopted a consolidation proposal. Two of the eight—Tampa, Florida, and Augusta, Georgia—have tried and failed on three successive occasions.

Why the civic reformers have had so little success in getting voters to approve consolidation proposals has been the subject of considerable debate. Some reformers place much of the blame on "selfish interests" that attempt to thwart consolidation efforts every step of the way from the initiation stage through the referendum campaign. In addition, the reformers often blame a poor showing at the polls on voter apathy, ignorance, and irrationality.

Such explanations tend to beg the question and turn out to be little more than excuses. "The world is made of selfish people— selfish if their interests are viewed from the perspectives of others."[7] Voter apathy is not unknown in the United States, but it fails to explain why the voters who do take the time to cast their ballots behave as they do. Charges of voter ignorance and irrationality amount to little more than casting derision upon those who vote against consolidation proposals. Ignorance is a relative term, and when it comes to highly value-laden issues like city-county consolidation, rationality is not restricted to one side of the controversy.

Other explanations of the difficulties encountered by the proponents of city-county consolidation either implicitly or explicitly place much of the blame on the reformers themselves. They have

Table 1. Consolidation Referenda since World War II

Community	Defeats	Passage	Community	Defeats	Passage
Baton Rouge, La.		1947	Roanoke, Va.	1969	
Newport News, Va.	1950	1957	Winchester, Va.	1969	
Hampton, Va.		1952	Brunswick, Ga.	1969	
Nashville, Tenn.	1958	1962	Charlottesville, Va.	1970	
Albuquerque, N.M.	1959, 1973		Pensacola, Fla.	1970	
Knoxville, Tenn.	1959		Anchorage, Alaska	1970, 1971	1975
Macon, Ga.	1960, 1972		Augusta, Ga.	1971, 1974, 1976	
Ravalli Co., Mont.	1960		Charlotte, N.C.	1971	
Durham, N.C.	1961, 1974		Tallahassee, Fla.	1971, 1973	
Richmond, Va.	1961		Bristol, Va.	1971	
Virginia Beach, Va.		1962	Sitka, Alaska		1971
S. Norfolk, Va.		1962	Columbia, S.C.	1972	
Memphis, Tenn.	1962, 1971		Lexington, Ky.		1972
Columbus, Ga.	1962	1970	Wilmington, N.C.	1973	
Chattanooga, Tenn.	1964, 1970		Sacramento, Cal.	1974	
Jacksonville, Fla.		1967	Charleston, S.C.	1974	
Tampa, Fla.	1967, 1970, 1972		Portland, Ore.	1974	
Juneau, Alaska		1969	Evansville, Ind.	1974	
Carson City, Nev.		1969	Salt Lake City, Utah	1974	
Athens, Ga.	1969, 1972		Ashland, Ky.	1974	

been accused of being politically naïve, overzealous in trying to use city-county consolidation to produce a complete "reform" of local systems of government, insensitive to the arguments of their opponents, and committed to a number of highly questionable assumptions about the metropolis and its people.

There is little question that the proponents of city-county consolidation have been consistently and overwhelmingly drawn from the middle and upper classes. They are usually backed by the Chamber of Commerce, the League of Women Voters, and other civic or business groups representing social and economic elites. Their major arguments, moreover, have been cast in terms of economy and efficiency in government, a concept that makes sense primarily to those used to thinking in terms of such managerial concepts as economies of scale, cost-benefit ratios, and long-range investment priorities.[8]

In addition, the civic reformers often assume that their arguments are self-evident and irrefutable. This leads to a distinct bias against getting involved in politics, often to the point of refusing to try to organize grass-roots support for consolidation proposals. The words of David Booth concerning the 1958 defeat of city-county consolidation in Nashville-Davidson County, Tennessee, illustrate this point: "Metro's proponents coasted along, without having to subject their views to the test of clever, documented and articulate criticism. Metro's desirability was generally accepted as self-evident, and no one really troubled to prove this. When, in the last week before the vote, the opposition unleashed its misleading propaganda, it was too late for the proponents to answer the allegations."[9] To underscore this point, Booth made the following observation about the successful city-county consolidation drive in Nashville four years later. "In 1958, the main failure of the pro-Metro forces was a failure to communicate with over half the population, or as the *Tennessean* stated, 'the lack of a block by block organization.' In 1962, the campaign was organized much more broadly and in greater depth. On both sides, it was as if the professionals and the politicians had taken over from the amateurs and do-gooders."[10]

Other observers feel that even if the proponents of city-county consolidation waged all-out campaigns based on arguments that might appeal to the average voter, they would not be able to improve substantially upon their won-lost record at the polls. These critics feel that the typical civic reformer tends to perceive the metropolis as a single social and economic entity whose major, if not sole, problem is one of having too many local political boundaries that have not kept pace with this reality.[11] It is at this point, the argument continues, that the assumptions of many civic reformers come into fundamental conflict with the findings of many urban experts. When these experts look at a metropolitan area they see, rather than a single socioeconomic entity, a "mosaic of social and economic worlds" based on differing social, economic, and life-style interests that tend to cluster in urban space. The people residing in each of these clusters, moreover, tend to develop well-defined perceptions of what is and what is not conducive to maintaining their social, economic, and life-style interests.[12]

Once the metropolis has been defined as a collection of spatially segregated social and economic groups, each fighting to maintain its identity and integrity, it can be argued that there are often sound reasons for many voters to oppose city-county consolidation attempts. This is especially true, it can be argued, when the spatial contours of the "mosaic of social worlds" happen to square with the legal boundaries of local governmental jurisdictions within an urban area. If a particular segment of the mosaic can have its own local government, it can exercise considerable control over such vital areas of public policy as zoning, taxation levels, and spending priorities. In such circumstances, it may not be illogical or irrational for certain segments of the metropolitan community to place a great deal of value on maintaining existing local government boundaries.[13]

Stated in their most general form, the arguments and findings of the urban experts are difficult to attack. Indeed, a number of scholars associated with the civic reform movement have conceded this point. Some have even helped to illuminate many of the empirical shortcomings of the traditional assumptions brought to bear on the question of city-county consolidation by the reformers.[14]

Serious problems arise, however, when the arguments and findings of the experts are stated in more precise terms. It is one thing to be able to demonstrate that the metropolis is a mosaic of social worlds. It is quite another matter to state with reasonable precision the dimensions along which the mosaic is organized in a particular metropolitan setting. Similarly, while it would appear from the record that many urban dwellers place considerable value on maintaining local governmental boundaries, there is little consistency in the findings to date concerning the conditions under which various types of boundary values become salient to those confronted with consolidation proposals.

One of the basic dimensions along which urban residents are supposed to organize their perceptions and reactions to consolidation proposals is "social distance." The general hypothesis has been that individuals are more likely to support city-county consolidation proposals when the existing units of government to be merged are or are perceived to be similar in socioeconomic or cultural terms. In such cases, social distance is assumed to be low, and those affected are presumably not called upon to support any serious restructuring of the social, economic, or cultural values of the premerger setting.

Such a hypothesis seems logical, but a careful search of the literature reveals several serious problems. The notion of social distance has been defined and measured in a variety of ways, making it extremely difficult to compare the findings of various researchers on the question. In addition, the findings to date, regardless of how social distance is defined and measured, are not very consistent.

For example, the concept of social distance has been defined in terms of social status differences as measured by class, income, occupation, and education. Some research findings support the popular contention that high social status areas tend to react negatively to the prospect of being politically and governmentally integrated with lower status areas. But it is also possible to cite findings that run counter to this. Hawkins, for example, discovered that "social differences increasingly in favor of the fringe" tended to be associated with "an *increasing* tendency for the fringe to vote *for* city-county consolidation (emphasis added).[15]

Other scholars define social distance in terms of life-style. Again, it is not difficult to find evidence that areas characterized as being committed to a familistic, child-oriented life-style tend to oppose political and governmental integration with less familistic areas.[16] Other studies, however, seem to suggest that this may not be the case. Indeed, one study suggests that the reverse may be true, that fringe areas with considerably higher levels of familism may actually support political integration with less familistic jurisdictions, including core cities.[17]

Scattered references also suggest the possibility that social-distance considerations are really drawn along racial lines. Again, the findings tend to be confusing. Some studies suggest that central-city blacks will oppose consolidation because they fear the political consequences of being inundated by white voters from the suburbs.[18] Yet sometimes a majority of central-city blacks has voted for consolidation. Similarly, one can find some evidence to show that central-city whites may, on occasion, vote to support consolidation in order to preclude a black take-over of the central-city government.[19] And it has been suggested that many white fringe dwellers have supported consolidation in order to preclude a black take-over of the central-city government, particularly where the black population of the central city was relatively large.[20] However, in a study of fringe voters in Augusta, Georgia, where there was a very real possibility that blacks would soon take over the central-city government if consolidation was defeated, it was discovered that such white voters may not always follow this pattern. In fact, it was discovered that even among those white fringe voters in Augusta who believed that blacks would soon take over the central-city government unless consolidation passed and also believed that this would be a "bad thing," the distribution of opinions on consolidation was an even 50-50 split.[21]

But social distance is not the only dimension along which voter attitudes toward consolidation can be organized. Some urban experts argue that what is really at stake whenever the question of city-county consolidation is raised is the kind of changes that such an arrangement will bring to the political and governmental system under which local residents are to live. The basic premise is that a proposal calling for substantial changes in existing "political arrangements . . . threatens (or is perceived as threatening) the political-governmental world that citizens, governmental employees and officials, and political leaders have learned to live with and like."[22]

Precisely what features of the "political-governmental world" are most salient to voters remains a matter of debate. Sometimes the line may be drawn in terms of a specific political personality, as in the case of some Nashville voters who reported in 1962 that their reactions to consolidation were related to their reactions to Nashville's colorful and controversial mayor, Ben West.[23] Other researchers have reported a more structurally oriented set of responses. For example, Marando discovered that support for consolidation proposals tended to increase as emphasis on district representation on the proposed council increased.[24] However, the findings concerning reactions to other structural features such as mayor-council versus council-manager forms of government are fragmentary and quite inconsistent.

The third basic set of explanations for voter reactions to consolidation proposals involves strictly economic considerations. The basic hypothesis has been that those who perceive higher taxes or fewer services under consolidation will tend to oppose it. All evidence to date seems to confirm the importance of tax-benefit considerations in structuring voter attitudes toward city-county consolidation. But it is not entirely clear what the conditions are under which voters will support or oppose consolidation on the basis of tax versus service considerations. After all, it is possible to support a change even if it will mean higher taxes if there is some hope of receiving additional or improved services. Similarly, it is conceivable that some voters prefer fewer or lower quality services regardless of how cheaply they are offered.

Several explanations can be given for the gaps and inconsistencies found in the literature concerning each of the three basic theories about voter reactions to consolidation proposals. According to one explanation, voters actually bring various combinations of social-distance, regime-government, and tax-benefit orientations to bear on the question of consolidating local governments. Consider, for example, an individual who believes that consolidation will result in: (a) few or no significant changes in life-style interests; (b) more responsive and representative government; and (c) higher taxes or fewer services. In social-distance terms, the voter in question is neutral. On the regime-government dimension, he is being pulled toward possibly supporting merger. And on the economic dimension, he is being pulled toward opposing the idea.[25]

Unfortunately, we do not have the kind of systematic data required to predict which of these three basic sets of sociopolitical orientations most voters are likely to follow when confronted with such attitudinal crosspressures. It is even more difficult to predict the distribution of pro-con attitudes toward consolidation that may prevail in a given consolidation setting once we discover which of these sociopolitical orientations is most salient. After all, it is possible for most voters in two different communities to follow, for example, their tax-benefit orientations and still render two different verdicts. If a majority feel that consolidation will produce more services for their tax dollar in one community, the measure is likely to pass. If, on the other hand, most voters in the other community feel that it will result in fewer or lower-quality services for their tax dollar, the idea is likely to be defeated.

Despite these limitations, we now know that voter reactions to city-county consolidation proposals involve a complex web of socioeconomic and political considerations. In fact, the more we learn about the nature of these complexities, the more interested we become in learning how certain situational factors may affect both the salience and the distribution of social-distance, regime-government, and tax-benefit orientations toward consolidation. We are again asking ourselves the same questions posed in some of the earlier and more descriptive case studies. Does the location, size, and composition of a community make a difference in the outcome of consolidation referenda? Does the number of existing units of local government or the relationship between existing political boundaries and the contours of the "mosaic of social worlds" help or impede the consolidation process? Do local issues other than merger ever affect the chance of securing voter approval for consolidation? If so, what impact do such issues as political scandal or threat of annexation have upon voters facing a merger referendum?

Although the answers to such questions remain quite tentative, it has become difficult to ignore the possible importance of certain situational factors upon the eventual outcome of consolidation efforts. Perhaps the best way to illustrate this point is to compare Lexington with the other communities that have attempted city-county consolidation since World War II in terms of those situational factors thought to play a crucial role in shaping voter reactions toward such proposals.

3

The Lexington Setting

LIKE MOST other communities that have held consolidation referenda since World War II, Lexington is in the southeastern region of
the United States. The significance of this is probably related less to
the social, economic, or cultural traits associated with the South
than to the fact that local governments in Kentucky are organized
according to the typical southern model in which there are only two
basic types of general-purpose government—counties and incorporated municipalities. Although it is not unusual to find more than
one incorporated municipality within a single southern county,
other types of general-purpose governments, such as townships, do
not complicate the problem of consolidating city and county governments.

It can be argued that the absence of general-purpose governments other than cities and counties helps to explain why most
consolidation referenda have been held in communities with the
southern model of local government. But it cannot explain why
some of these consolidation efforts have succeeded while others
have failed.

Some observers have tried to explain the voting record in terms
of variations in the size of referenda communities. Considerable
variation in population size does exist, although the largest consolidation settings do not rank among the nation's very large urban
areas: the range is from 5,965 (Sitka-Greater Sitka, Alaska) to
718,777 (Memphis-Shelby County, Tennessee).

When placed on this continuum, the Lexington setting appears to
be quite typical. At the time the merger proposal was submitted to

the voters of Lexington and Fayette County in November 1972, the population stood at 174,323. This fell very close to the average population size (197,513) of all communities that attempted consolidation referenda between the end of World War II and November 1972.

In terms of victories and defeats, however, the Lexington population size begins to look a bit less typical. While Lexington's population in 1972 was only slightly higher than the average "winner" community up to that point (137,919), a closer examination of the distribution of "winner" communities reveals that the odds against obtaining voter approval were considerably higher in those communities with population of 100,000 or more. Of the sixteen merger attempts in settings with populations under 100,000, half were successful. In contrast, of the twenty-seven attempts in cities larger than 100,000, only four, or less than 15 percent, succeeded. Lexington not only stands out as one of the relatively few communities with a population of over 100,000 to secure voter approval of a consolidation proposal, but it became the third-largest community to do so between World War II and November 1972. It was the second-largest community to do so the first time the question was put on the ballot.

Perhaps the full import of Lexington's place on the population scale can be better understood if we examine the basic assumptions underlying much of the concern over population size found in the literature. One of these assumptions has been that as population size increases, so will the likelihood that the proponents of city-county merger will have to contend with a larger number of local units of government. Second, it has been argued that the larger the community, the more complicated the "mosaic of social worlds" becomes. Both the number of local governments and the complexity of the "mosaic" have been posited as key variables affecting the outcome of city-county consolidation efforts.

Lexington seemed quite typical of most referenda settings in having to contend with only two units of government in the pre-merger environment. However, many communities (both larger and smaller than Lexington) with only two basic units of local government have failed to obtain voter support for a city-county consolidation proposal. Nor should it be forgotten that both settings larger than Lexington where victories were scored before 1972 had higher "fragmentation" scores—Jacksonville, Florida, with six units and Nashville, Tennessee, with eight.

This does not deny the proposition that the larger the community, the more likely it becomes that the proponents of city-county consolidation will have to contend with more governmental fragmentation. Nor does it suggest that the presence of only one city within a single county was not an asset in the Lexington case. It merely questions the utility of the governmental fragmentation implications of the population argument in explaining won-lost records. It is quite conceivable that even among those communities in states with the typical southern model of local government, only those with relatively low fragmentation scores ever reach the point of holding a consolidation referendum. If so, we are left with little more than an explanation for the concentration of merger *efforts* in such communities.

Nevertheless, there does seem to be a relationship between population size and the won-lost record in consolidation referenda. This has led some researchers to argue that the effects of increased population size can best be understood in terms of its tendency to complicate the "mosaic of social worlds." The underlying assumption is that increases in population tend to result in larger numbers of racial, ethnic, life-style, and socioeconomic subcommunities seeking to protect and preserve their identities. The more numerous and more varied these spatially defined subcommunities become, the argument continues, the more difficult it becomes to secure voter approval for an area-wide, consolidated government.[1]

A key factor affecting the validity of this argument, however, is the extent to which local political boundaries correspond with the contours of the mosaic of social worlds. It may be quite logical for voters in one social world to resist attempts to merge them politically with a quite different social world if they also happen to have their own unit of government with the power to determine such matters as zoning, taxation levels, and spending priorities. Conversely, voters from differing social worlds may find consolidation less threatening if existing political boundaries cut across the

mosaic in a haphazard fashion. In such cases, it becomes more difficult for voters to perceive that existing political boundaries serve to
protect the interests of any particular social world.

Obviously, this entire line of argument depends on how the concept of social worlds is defined. The more specific the definition,
the less likely it becomes that there will be much correspondence
between social and political worlds. In addition, relatively low governmental fragmentation scores such as those observed in communities that have held consolidation referenda since World War II
can also affect the correspondence between social and political
worlds. Nevertheless, one would be hard pressed to find another
consolidation setting in which existing political boundaries cut
across the mosaic of social worlds in a more erratic fashion than
those in Lexington prior to the 1972 merger referendum.

Although most tourist brochures portray it as the Thoroughbred
horse capital of the world, there is more to Lexington than famous
horse farms. It is also a rapidly growing metropolitan area with an
estimated population (1975) of more than 200,000 people. Between 1940 and the last official census in 1970, its population grew
from 79,800 to 174,323. Between 1960 and 1970, its population
increased by 32 percent, making it the fourteenth-fastest-growing
Standard Metropolitan Statistical Area (SMSA) in the country.

Much of this growth was stimulated by the arrival of several
major manufacturing firms such as IBM shortly after the end of
World War II. An equally important factor has been the expansion
of the University of Kentucky throughout the postwar period. In
addition, a major health care industry has been built around the
University of Kentucky Medical Center, the Veterans Administration Hospital, the Shriners Hospital for Crippled Children, and
several large general hospital facilities.[2]

As might be expected, rapid growth left its mark on the mosaic
of social worlds in Lexington. A wide variety of occupational
groups was imported to operate the major growth industries and
related service sectors of the local economy. And those who moved
into the Lexington area to fill these needs tended to cluster in certain sections of town according to income levels, and often accord-

ing to occupations. Thus most blue-collar and lower status white-collar workers tended to settle in the north end of town, while most incoming managerial and professional workers gravitated to the burgeoning suburbs to the south.

What made the Lexington merger setting unique, however, was its crazy city-county boundary. After decades of piecemeal annexation, the city of Lexington included a wide variety of socioeconomic worlds, many of them virtually surrounded by similar kinds of areas that happened to remain in the county. The city boundary reached out along narrow strips of land bordering arterial roads to embrace particular subdivisions, while completely bypassing large chunks of equally built-up neighborhoods, often of similar socioeconomic status. In many instances the first one or two properties on a particular street were in the city, with the next two or three in the county, and then several more in the city (see Figure 1).

There is, however, another dimension along which the concept of social worlds can be drawn. That dimension is race. From the underlying assumptions of the social-distance argument, it would appear that the optimal setting for invoking a strictly racial response to the question of city-county consolidation would be one in which: (a) most blacks resided in one of the political units involved; (b) the percentage of blacks in that unit is relatively large (perhaps 30 to 50 percent or more); and (c) all other units of government in the area are predominantly white.

Under such circumstances, we should find central-city blacks *opposing* consolidation in order to prevent a dilution of their voting power and to maximize their chances of taking over the central-city governments. Conversely, we should also expect to find central-city whites voting *for* the merger proposal simply to preclude any potential black take-over. Finally, in order to meet the underlying assumptions of the social-distance argument when stated in racial terms, we ought to find those members of the white "social world" living outside the central-city boundary ready to come to the aid of their white counterparts in the city, particularly where there is a real chance that the city government might fall into the hands of black politicians. To paraphrase Sloan and French, the "risk of for-

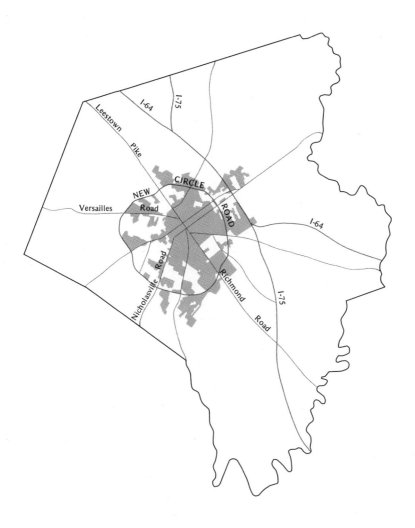

Figure 1. Political Jurisdictions
of Lexington and Fayette County, 1971

feiting the city's government to blacks may well be sufficient to swing many white suburbanites to a [promerger] position."[3]

Although only a few of the consolidation settings since World War II conform to the rather rigorous conditions outlined above, about half of them contained central cities with black populations in the 30 to 50 percent range.[4] Another 20 percent had central cities that were more than one-fifth black at the time the merger question appeared on the ballot. And with the exception of Baton Rouge, where the city was 28 percent black and the area outside the city was 52 percent black, most of these merger settings with sizable central-city black populations also had fringe areas that were predominantly white. In varying degrees, then, almost three-fourths of all merger settings since World War II came close to the optimal conditions for invoking a serious racial confrontation over consolidation.

It is difficult to find hard evidence with which to confirm or reject the various hypotheses found in the literature concerning the racial implications of the social-distance argument. A number of inferences about the impact of racial considerations on central-city blacks have been drawn on the basis of aggregate voting returns. For the most part, these findings suggest that central-city blacks tend to resist being politically and governmentally consolidated with predominantly white fringe areas. It has even been suggested that in most cases this tendency produces large majorities against consolidation proposals among central-city blacks.

This seemed to be the case in Augusta, Georgia, during the 1971 consolidation referendum. The vote in the city, which was slightly more than 50 percent black, was a close 6,415 in favor of merger and 6,498 against. An examination of the vote by precincts, how-ever, reveals that the vote went overwhelmingly against merger in predominantly black areas, while almost all of the "Yes" vote was recorded in white areas of the city.

However, Sloan and French, who studied the voting returns of central-city black precincts in two settings that also came very close to satisfying the optimal conditions outlined above, discovered some rather striking differences in the level of black opposition to merger in Nashville (1958) and Jacksonville (1967). While the opposition to merger increased in both settings as the racial composition of central-city precincts became increasingly black, solid majorities against merger were recorded only in the Nashville setting. In Jacksonville, where over 40 percent of the central-city population was black, a "healthy majority of black voters approved consolidation."[5]

Sloan and French concluded that one of the major differences between the 1958 Nashville and the Jacksonville settings was that in the latter there was a good chance that, should merger fail, the city would embark upon a massive annexation program. Annexation meant taking into the city a large number of fringe areas that were over 90 percent white, with no change in the at-large system of representation employed in the city of Jacksonville. Under annexation the at-large concept would be applied to larger and larger areas that were destined to be less and less black.

At least the merger proposal in Jacksonville promised that the at-large system of representation employed by the city would be replaced with a predominantly single-member district system under which at least three of the fourteen district representatives would be elected from mainly black areas. And when a number of white leaders seemed prepared to support black candidates for some of the five at-large seats on the new merged government council, the choice seemed clear. "Black leaders sought the best deal they could get," and in Jacksonville that seemed to be merger.[6]

There have been other situations where a majority of central-city blacks have supported consolidation. In Charlotte, North Carolina, for example, "the only precincts returning majorities for the [consolidation] charter were either black or racially mixed."[7] Although blacks constituted less than 20 percent of the central-city population in this case, they seemed to react favorably to consolidation as a means to replace the at-large system of representation with a predominantly single-member district arrangement for both the local government council and the school board.[8] Once again, however, the Charlotte example stands as an exception to the general rule.

The evidence concerning white reactions to the racial implications of consolidation proposals is quite fragmentary and often inconclusive. It can be argued, for example, that central-city whites in the 1971 Augusta situation voted along racial lines as much as their black central-city counterparts. But this observation is based on aggregate data which cannot measure whether racism was the underlying variable that produced this voting pattern.

Survey data gathered by Schley Lyons seem to indicate that the school-busing decision handed down by federal courts shortly before the 1971 consolidation vote in Charlotte had an impact upon white voter reactions. During the months preceding the consolidation referendum there was mounting opposition to the court order, under the leadership of a group of white citizens known as the Concerned Parents Association (CPA). It did not take long for the CPA to take aim at the proposed consolidation with its provisions concerning district representation, especially on the school board. The link had been forged, and the controversy raged in the press for weeks. Nevertheless, Lyons found only a modest correlation between white attitudes toward integration and attitudes toward consolidation. Although he concluded that the "busing issue was clearly tapping into feelings other than simple opposition to mixing the races," the basic thrust of his findings clearly suggested that factors other than race or busing contributed to the overwhelming anticonsolidation vote cast by both central-city and suburban whites.[9]

Considerable attention has been given to the racial implications of consolidation proposals in other communities because they help to shed some light on the situation that prevailed in the Lexington case. On at least two counts, for example, the Lexington setting conformed to the kind of optimal situation that is seemingly conducive to invoking race as a major issue in the consolidation process. First, most of the nonwhite population in Fayette County, 85 percent to be precise, was concentrated in the city of Lexington in 1972. Second, the area outside the city boundary was predominantly white. Indeed, the total fringe area was almost 95 percent white, and most of the built-up, suburban areas immediately adjacent to the city could be described as "lily white."

However, the central-city black population in Lexington fell considerably short of the 30 to 50 percent range suggested by the social-distance theory. In fact, out of a total city population of

108,137 people in 1970, there were only 18,909 blacks. Clearly, Lexington was not in the same category as Augusta, Nashville, or Jacksonville in terms of racial composition. Nor did it rank among the approximately 50 percent of all merger settings since World War II that had central cities with more than 30 percent blacks. By the same token, Lexington was not an Albuquerque, New Mexico, or a Winchester, Virginia, where nonwhites were almost nonexistent in either the central city or the fringe areas. It was not a Baton Rouge where central-city blacks constituted 28 percent of the total city population and almost two-thirds of the population living outside the city, nor a Carson City, Nevada, with a city population of less than 5 percent nonwhite and a fringe area made up of over 35 percent nonwhites. And it certainly was not a Memphis or a Chattanooga where the city-fringe distribution of blacks was almost even.

The consolidation settings most comparable to Lexington in racial terms were Roanoke, Knoxville, and Tampa. Although the voters had rejected consolidation in Roanoke and Knoxville, and on three different occasions in Tampa, little is known about the impact of racial considerations in those settings. It therefore became necessary for the proponents of consolidation in Lexington to consider two basic questions. First, was there anything about the distribution of the races in Lexington and Fayette County that might invoke a racial response to the merger question on the part of central-city blacks, central-city whites, or white fringe dwellers? Second, were there any extenuating circumstances such as those found in Jacksonville or Charlotte that could affect the direction and intensity of racial considerations on the part of any of these groups?

It was understood from the outset that central-city blacks could conceivably hold the key to success or failure in a tight referendum contest. Thus, considerable attention was given to the question of how central-city blacks in Lexington might react to the idea of consolidation. On the one hand, notice was taken of the general pattern of black rejection of the idea. Yet, several things about the Lexington situation pointed toward a more positive response.

Central-city blacks had little to gain by opposing merger. Although a vast majority of blacks in the total community lived in the city, they were nowhere near the stage of electing a black mayor on their own, or even electing a majority to the city commission within the prevailing at-large system of representation without substantial help from the white community. The worst they could expect from merger was a slight dilution of their voting power. Even this had to be balanced against two other factors present in the Lexington setting.

As will be noted later, there was a very real possibility that, should merger fail, the city would begin annexing large chunks of predominantly white fringe areas. Second, if merger failed, it meant a continuation of an at-large system of representation. At least the merger proposal called for twelve of the fifteen members of the new "metro" council to be elected from single-member districts, and the districts were to be drawn to insure that two and possibly three seats would go to black candidates.

On the other side of the coin, whites in Lexington were not confronted with any objective threat of a black take-over of the central-city government. Even the most bigoted white voter could expect only the most trivial dilution of black voting power under merger. And with annexation in the wind, there was no reason to support merger as the *only* way to dilute the black presence in Lexington.

All in all, there seemed to be little fodder for a major racial confrontation over city-county merger in the Lexington setting. At least the objective implications of merger for central-city blacks seemed to be loaded in favor of their supporting the proposed charter as the best deal available. And there seemed to be nothing in the situational setting that could objectively lead whites on either side of the city line to support or resist such a move on strictly racial grounds.

In addition to such factors as size, location, governmental fragmentation, and the correspondence between various social and political worlds, one must consider the potential impact of miscellaneous threats to the status quo, ranging from charges of political corruption against incumbent public officials during the consolidation process to court-ordered busing prior to a consolidation referendum. Another threat to the status quo, and one of particular importance to Lexington, is annexation. Sloan and French were convinced that one of the things that led central-city blacks in Jacksonville to vote for consolidation in 1967 was a perceived threat that a major annexation program would be implemented if consolidation failed.

Threatened annexation can have an impact on other voters as well. David Booth, for example, attributed much of the difference between the 1958 defeat and the 1962 passage of merger in Nashville to an annexation controversy. Following the 1958 referendum, the city of Nashville began a massive annexation program. In 1960, the city annexed over 50 square miles of mostly residential areas on its fringe. The move increased the city's population by more than 82,000 and more than doubled its land area.[10]

According to Booth, the experience with annexation between 1958 and the 1962 merger campaign had a profound impact on two important sets of voters. Although the city had voted in favor of merger in 1958, the city electorate had been enlarged considerably during the period between 1958 and 1962. In the recently annexed parts of the city the vote ran heavily in favor of merger in 1962. The vote in the newly annexed areas ran "six and seven to one in favor of consolidation, yielding an over-all figure for the city of 21,064 in favor to 15,599 against."[11]

The annexation controversy following the 1958 defeat of merger in the Nashville setting seemed to have an equally profound effect on those who still lived outside the city when the 1962 merger proposal was put to a vote. While the areas outside the city had voted heavily against merger in 1958, in 1962 they voted 15,914 in favor of consolidation and 12,514 against. Booth attributed much of the shift in the fringe vote between 1958 and 1962 to the fear of further annexation by the city. For these voters the issue was clearly one of "whether [they] wanted to be liable to annexation at any time, yet receive no guarantee of better services; or whether . . . to adopt Metro, which guaranteed services within one year after any property became part of the urban services district."[12]

It is difficult to establish the precise impact that the threat of annexation may have had upon the pattern of success or failure observed among the fifty-six merger referenda conducted since World War II. The problem seems to lie in the term "threat."

Obviously, a "threat" of annexation is in the eyes of the beholder, and we simply do not have sufficient survey data to test whether or not annexation was perceived as a factor in the politics of merger in a variety of settings. The best we can do is to rely on the scattered references to the subject found in the essentially descriptive case study literature.

The arguments and findings presented in the case study literature, however, do allow one to assert that annexation seems to have played a very important role in at least five of the twelve *successful* merger campaigns conducted between 1947 and 1972. Furthermore, there is some reason to believe that in these five cases annexation had a profound impact on the voting behavior of central-city blacks, central-city whites who may have been recently annexed by the city, and fringe voters generally. In each case, the available information points toward the conclusion that past or threatened annexation efforts on the part of the central city tend to generate support for city-county consolidation.

Mention has already been made of the court-ordered annexation plan in the Lexington setting and its implications for central-city blacks. Several additional details about this plan and its possible impact upon other sets of voters in the Lexington merger setting are now in order.

Before passage of the merger-enabling law in 1970, the only legal alternative available to those interested in squaring local governmental boundaries with the social and economic realities of the outward explosion of urban population was annexation. The city of Lexington had tried on several occasions after World War II to annex all of the growing, built-up areas on its periphery. On each occasion, property owners in the areas affected took their objections to court.[13] On each occasion, the city retreated to a position of "voluntary annexation" on a piecemeal basis. In fact, it was this policy that led to the "crazy boundary" seen in Figure 1.

In September of 1968 an independent research organization hired by the city of Lexington issued a report recommending that the city annex all of the remaining built-up fringe. Under the proposal, the city would have more than doubled its territory and almost doubled its population size.[14] Except for several minor points, the city commission adopted the report in the form of an annexation ordinance several months later.

Protests were quickly filed with the local circuit court by property owners affected by the ordinance. However, on this occasion less than 50 percent of the affected property owners remonstrated, and the burden of proof was thus placed on them to prove that being annexed would do them irreparable harm. Everything seemed to be in favor of those interested in replacing the irregular city-county boundary with a more rational set of jurisdictional boundaries based on the pattern of urbanization in this rapidly growing area.

Then came the municipal election of November 1968. Campaigning on the one issue of opposition to the recently passed city sewer tax, a faction led by Thomas Underwood won three of the four seats on the City Commission. In control of three out of five votes on the commission (the fifth member being the mayor, whose term ran for two more years), the Underwood faction proceeded to take over city affairs, including the city's position before the local courts regarding the 1968 annexation order.

The details of the ensuing court battle over annexation were interesting from a purely political standpoint.[15] The Underwood faction ultimately consented to a compromise annexation plan that was accepted by the fringe opponents. It contained three basic elements: first, the city consented to rescind its 1968 annexation ordinance; second, it agreed that the city would not undertake any annexation in most of the area covered by the 1968 ordinance except on a voluntary basis until 1975; third, it agreed that, except for possible voluntary annexations, the city would not encroach upon the remaining areas scheduled for annexation until 1980.

The court agreed to this compromise and handed down an order forbidding any annexations other than purely voluntary ones in the two designated areas until 1975 and 1980 respectively. But in so doing, the court exempted any annexation proceedings affecting these two areas following the 1975 and 1980 deadlines from any appeal on the part of local property owners. The city was free to implement the 1968 ordinance without legal interference in two stages. It could take in most of the built-up areas in 1975, and the rest after 1980.

It was within this context that the city-county merger effort was initiated by a group of local citizens in the summer of 1970. By the time the merger question was placed before the local electorate in November of 1972, the reality of the court order regarding annexation was less than three years away. Furthermore, the Underwood faction on the City Commission that had agreed to the delaying compromise had been soundly defeated the previous year. Unless it could recapture control of the city government during the 1973 election, a possibility that could occur only if the merger proposal failed, it would not be around to thwart the city's option to pursue the implications of the annexation order.[16] Thus, the situation in November of 1972 pointed toward either a merger of the city and county governments, or a very high probability that the city would annex large chunks of fringe territory in the very near future.

The objective choice facing central-city blacks was whether to vote against merger in order to preclude an immediate but slight dilution of their voting power, or support merger on the grounds that it promised to replace the city's at-large system with a predominantly district system of representation. The first option, however, meant risking inundation by more white voters who would be brought into the existing at-large system by annexation. The latter offered a virtual guarantee that at least two and possibly three of the twelve district seats on the fifteen-member council would go to black candidates.

There were also several objective considerations facing fringe voters. Previous experience suggested that being annexed by the city meant an immediate and very substantial property tax increase with no guarantee when additional city services would be provided.[17] Although a 1969 amendment to the state constitution permitted cities to vary property tax rates to reflect variations in the kind and level of services rendered, no city in the state had yet exercised this option.[18]

A variable tax rate tied to the level of services rendered was a major and obvious part of the proposed merger proposal. Indeed, the Lexington proposal went beyond other consolidation charters by providing that no additional property taxes would be imposed on fringe residents until additional urban services were actually installed. Moreover, there were provisions to allow various areas to obtain one or more additional urban services without having to pay the full tax rate imposed on those receiving the full range of urban services.

Annexation was not the only threat to the status quo at the time merger came up for a vote in the Lexington setting. There was also the question of Lexington's future legal status as a city of the second class. According to the 1970 census, Lexington's population was 107,944, and the state constitution clearly required the state legislature to classify all incorporated municipalities with more than 100,000 people as first-class cities.[19] While the legislature had often ignored the mandate to reclassify cities according to population gains or losses, Lexington's status was in question, and there were those in the community who were insisting that the legislature declare it a city of the first class.[20]

Those backing merger cautioned the 1972 General Assembly against any hasty reclassification based on the 1970 census returns on the grounds that the state enabling legislation allowing for the merger of city and county governments specifically excluded counties containing first-class cities. Designating Lexington a first-class city at that point would have wiped out almost two years of effort and deprived the local electorate of a chance to decide whether it wanted merger or not.[21] In the end the delay was won. But it seemed clear to most observers that if merger failed, there would be renewed efforts to reclassify Lexington in accordance with the constitution during the next session of the legislature, commencing in January 1974.

Becoming a first-class city implied more than a simple change in labels. It might mean a shift from the "manager" form of government to the mayor-council form. A law on the books that had been endorsed by the Underwood faction said, in effect, that a second-class city with a "manager" form of government could retain that form upon becoming a city of the first class. Although this statute was designed to exempt Lexington from the long-standing legal requirement that all first-class cities adopt the mayor-council form of government, there was some concern that the courts would declare it unconstitutional on the grounds that it was "special legislation."

Should the law be found unconstitutional, Lexington would be forced to make several major changes in its governmental system upon being reclassified as a first-class city. Not only would it have to shift from the manager to the mayor-council system, but its five-member City Commission would have to be replaced with a twelve-member council. Local elections would have to be conducted on a partisan rather than a nonpartisan basis. Finally, its system of representation would have to be modified. Candidates for the twelve-member first-class city council, while elected at large, would have to reside in specified districts rather than anywhere in the city as was the case in Lexington under second-class city status.[22]

Even if the courts allowed Lexington to retain its manager form of government, its reclassification as a first-class city would bring a host of other changes. The civil service law for first-class cities, for example, exempted numerous positions that were covered in Lexington. First-class cities were obligated by statute to perform a wide variety of welfare services that were either not given in Lexington or were the sole responsibility of the county government. Furthermore, Kentucky had never had a first-class city other than Louisville, and the statute books were full of items designed primarily for the Louisville situation. Those pertaining to the regulation of ports seemed especially irrelevant to land-locked Lexington.

At the time the question was being debated in Lexington, it was difficult for the proponents of merger to assess the possible impact of this additional threat to the status quo upon their chances of success. Up to that time the voters in no other merger setting had faced this kind of alternative. The best any prognosticator could do was to rely upon logic and intuition. On both counts it seemed plausible to argue that city voters and those scheduled to become part of the city under annexation might find the provisions for reorganizing local government under a homegrown merger proposal more acceptable than the provisions that would inevitably result under state law should Lexington be declared a first-class city.

On a number of counts then Lexington seemed an ideal place to attempt city-county consolidation. There were only two units of local government in the area, and the boundary separating city and county residents wandered across the mosaic of social worlds in an extremely haphazard fashion. It had a relatively small black population that was unlikely to prompt a racial confrontation over merger. And there were at least two major threats to the status quo on the horizon other than merger—annexation and first-class city status for the city of Lexington.

4

The First Steps

No matter how favorable the situational factors may appear to city-county consolidation advocates in a particular community, several major hurdles must be passed before the final test can be run at the polls. One of these is to get a board or commission established and functioning with the legal authority to draft a plan or charter for establishing a merged government to be submitted to the local electorate. Another is to ensure that such a commission is not thwarted from completing its task before the voters have a chance to speak.

Unfortunately, little is known about these steps in the merger process. Scattered references are available concerning the types of individuals and groups who tend to support the creation of charter commissions. It is even possible to glean from the case study materials some insight into the various legal procedures that have been followed in creating a number of such commissions. Generally missing, however, is solid information about the politics of creating and maintaining such commissions. When it comes to who gets "what, when and how" at this stage in the process, the literature remains essentially mute.[1]

The Lexington experience provides an opportunity to examine this much neglected aspect of the merger process, and it also offers an excellent chance to compare, within a single setting, the effects of a hostile and a supportive political environment upon the preparation of a merger charter.

It would appear that the basic pattern of activity leading to the creation of a charter commission in Lexington was quite typical of that found in many other merger settings. A period during which various civic groups in the community sponsored discussions of the idea was followed by efforts on the part of local spokesmen to obtain the necessary legal authority from the state to allow the community to proceed formally with city-county merger. Once this was accomplished, steps were taken in the community to establish a charter commission.

The general impression one gets from reading such case study materials as those supplied by Temple is that each of these preliminary steps unfolds as part of a single movement led by a well-defined set of actors.[2] The popular view is that local civic clubs, often led by the Chamber of Commerce, sponsor programs and discussions on the virtues of merger, lead the drive to obtain state legislative support for enabling legislation, and then engage in a concerted effort to get a local charter commission established. Other individuals and groups may join in helping to promote one or more of these activities, but only in response to the leadership given by the Chamber of Commerce and its allies.

Whether this impression squares with reality in most merger situations is not known. It does not, however, square with the reality of the Lexington experience, where an almost accidental convergence of events and activities on the part of different groups marked the completion of these three steps leading to the creation of a charter commission.

Step one was carried out in Lexington as prescribed by the conventional wisdom. The Chamber of Commerce and the Rotary Club had sponsored a number of programs over the years on the subject of city-county consolidation. Speakers were invited from Nashville, Jacksonville, Baton Rouge, and other communities that had experienced merger to preach the gospel of economy and efficiency through consolidation. The local League of Women Voters held study sessions on the question. And the local Chamber eventually sponsored a trip to Jacksonville to see the advantages of merger in action.[3]

None of these groups, however, can be directly linked to the securing of a legal basis for proceeding with city-county merger. That task was left almost entirely to one man acting on his own, as a member of the Fayette County delegation in the lower house of the General Assembly. Representative Bart Peak, who says that his interest in the consolidation of city and county governments grew out of his experience as Fayette County judge, entered the state legislature in 1952. During his tenure in the legislature he thought about ways to write a city-county consolidation bill that would be consistent with the state constitution. But little came of these efforts, and nothing was done.

During the 1970 session of the General Assembly, Peak turned to Representative William McCann, a young colleague from Fayette County, for support. Together they sought the assistance of the Legislative Research Commission in drafting a bill to allow counties containing cities of the first or second class to merge their city and county governments into an "Urban County Government."

House Bill 543 was not widely debated or publicized. Several suburban Louisville legislators expressed reservations about including counties containing first-class cities, but they were unable to block the Peak-McCann proposal in the House. In the Senate, however, the delegation from Louisville and Jefferson County managed to tie it up in committee. But Peak and McCann quickly consented to an amendment eliminating the reference to counties containing cities of the first class. With that, the bill was released from the Senate committee and was passed by both houses during the waning hours of the 60-day session of the 1970 General Assembly. Shortly thereafter it was signed into law by the governor, along with a host of other routine bills.[4]

Neither Peak nor McCann, however, returned to Lexington proclaiming the victory they had won. No news conferences were held to announce the provisions of the newly enacted legislation. No attempts were made to interest the Chamber of Commerce, the Rotary Club, or any other group in seizing upon the opportunity provided by the bill to circulate petitions to force the city and county governments to appoint a "representative commission" to devise a "comprehensive plan" of "Urban County Government."[5]

There was, in short, a leadership vacuum in Lexington so far as merger was concerned following the passage of the Peak-McCann bill. After years of speeches and programs sponsored by major civic groups and after a seemingly independent crusade by Peak and McCann to secure a legal basis for proceeding with the creation of a charter commission, nothing was done by the groups and individuals mentioned up to this point.

There was, however, a small band of citizens who had been meeting on a rather informal basis since late 1969. In February 1970, about the time the Peak-McCann bill was before the state legislature, the group adopted the name "Governmental Options" (GO). The timing was purely coincidental and had nothing to do with the question of merger. In fact, the expressed purpose of the group was to be a "friendly critic of local governmental bodies."[6]

Although the concerns of its various members were quite diffuse, much of the raison d'être for GO grew out of the election and subsequent behavior of Tom Underwood and two of his associates as members of the five-member Lexington City Commission. In fact, two of the original members of the group, Jack Reeves and Edgar Wallace, had been defeated as independent candidates for seats on the City Commission during the 1969 contest.[7] Many of the other members were supporters of Reeves and/or Wallace, or open opponents of the Underwood team. A few were county residents who, although ineligible to vote in city races, were deeply disturbed by the turn of events in Lexington following the 1969 municipal election.

The Underwood faction took office in January 1970. It quickly became apparent that this three-member voting bloc was determined to stick together on more than the sewer-tax repeal they had promised in their campaign. Spending rose rapidly with little regard for budgetary considerations, and nothing was done to check the obvious shift toward some of the most blatant political favoritism to cross the local political scene in years. The entire style of city politics had changed from the quiet shenanigans of the "downtown establishment" to an openly discussed system of alleged corruption and mismanagement. Long before he was indicted and tried on charges of accepting bribes and conspiracy to commit bribery in 1971, Tom Underwood had left his mark on the community.[8]

Concerned as they were over the course of events in Lexington following the November 1969 municipal election, the members of GO found themselves completely frustrated over what to do about the situation. As time slipped by, it became more and more obvious that the group could not establish itself as a viable political force by monitoring the meetings of a wide variety of city and county boards and commissions. Nor was it making much headway as a "friendly critic of local governmental bodies" by clipping newspaper articles on the antics of the Underwood administration.

The records of the group are not very precise, mainly because every meeting tended to skip back and forth over numerous topics in the search for some consensus on what to do next. As a member of GO, however, the author can attest to the development of a general feeling that the group had spread itself too thin. In the early months of 1970, more and more discussion was given to the question of how to focus the energy and attention of the group on a single project that would (a) embrace most of the diverse concerns of its members and (b) have some chance of transforming the group into a recognized, action-oriented force in local affairs.

It was during one of the many discussions on the future thrust and purpose of GO that the author mentioned the recently enacted Peak-McCann bill. Few of those present had given any thought to the matter before. Most were aware that the massive annexation ordinance passed in the last days of the previous city administration was being challenged in the courts and that the Underwood faction seemed amenable to some sort of compromise to delay its implementation. But few of the members present were aware of the Peak-McCann bill. Some were not entirely sure what city-county consolidation meant, or how it differed from annexation.

In subsequent meetings the provisions of the bill were explained, and the general concept of merger was contrasted with the essential features of annexation and metropolitan federation. It soon became apparent that merger was precisely the kind of project GO had been looking for. It was sufficiently comprehensive in scope to embrace virtually all of the policy concerns of various members, including planning and zoning, urban renewal, sanitary sewers, police and fire protection, parks, and libraries. It held the prospect of completely altering the local system of government, which meant that it could be used to challenge the existence of the Underwood regime. And under the provisions of the Peak-McCann bill, there was something concrete that a group the size of GO could do, namely lead a campaign to secure enough names on a petition to force the City Commission and the Fiscal Court to appoint a merger charter commission.

By summer of 1970 the group had decided to sponsor the petition drive. According to KRS 67A.020–.040 (the Peak-McCann bill), the task was as follows:

Upon a petition filed with the county clerk and signed by a number of registered voters equal to 5 per cent of voters of the county voting in the immediate past general election, and, upon additional petitions equal to the number of municipal corporations within the county, filed with the county clerk and signed by a number of . . . voters equal to 5 per cent of voters of each municipal corporation, voting in the immediate past general election, requesting a referendum be held on the question of adopting the urban county form of government, the fiscal court and the council of the largest city within the county *shall appoint a representative commission composed of not less than twenty (20) citizens which shall devise a comprehensive plan of urban county government.* [Emphasis added]

Because of the wording of the law, the group decided to draft two petitions. One petition was for qualified and registered voters of the city of Lexington, the only incorporated municipality in Fayette County. The other was for county voters. Since city voters were also members of the county electorate, they were asked to sign *both* petitions. That way they could contribute to the five percent quota for both the city and the county.

It was also decided to avoid a time-consuming door-to-door petition campaign. GO simply announced that it was sponsoring a merger petition drive and invited all interested persons and groups to help circulate the petitions.[9] A number of individuals called to offer their help, including several who were active in the League of Women Voters and other civic groups, but no organized civic club involvement was forthcoming. The members of GO, with the help of a handful of interested citizens, conducted the drive.

At no time were there more than twenty-five or thirty people actively working on the petition drive. By scheduling talks before various groups, setting up booths in various business establishments and shopping malls, and assigning people to stand outside super-markets and on busy streets to solicit signatures, these few workers managed to get the requisite number of signatures on both sets of petitions. It took several months, and by the time the petitions were formally filed with the county clerk on November 10, the 1970 general election had been held. Although that off-year election reduced the number of names needed under the law, the totals on both petitions were in excess of the larger number required had the heated 1969 contest been the base line as originally contemplated.

The project was a major undertaking for a group whose members, despite their seemingly elite status in terms of income and education, were not part of the existing political power structure.[10] This is not to suggest that the members of GO initiated the merger effort in Lexington for reasons that were totally different from those generally articulated by chambers of commerce and other more traditional promerger groups. According to a survey of its members taken after the merger referendum in 1972, all members continued to support merger even though Tom Underwood and his two cronies had been soundly defeated at the polls during the 1971 municipal election. More important, the overwhelming majority reported that they had done so for such traditional civic-reform reasons as "economy and efficiency in government," "better planning for orderly growth," or "more responsive and representative government."[11]

Thus, despite the disjointed and uncoordinated efforts of various groups and individuals during the preliminary stages leading up to the creation of the Lexington-Fayette County Merger Commission, there was nothing to preclude the formation of a combined effort to complete the task at hand. Although GO virtually ceased to exist as an organization shortly after the petition drive was completed in November of 1970, its members continued to work for merger in a variety of ways. Two of its members were appointed to the merger commission at the outset, and a third member was eventually appointed to fill a vacancy. In addition, the Chamber of Commerce and the Rotary Club seized upon the merger issue as soon as the charter commission became a reality. Both local newspapers began to display an interest in the project by endorsing first the concept of merger and eventually the proposed charter. Once the petition drive was completed and the charter commission appointed, the pattern of organized support for merger in Lexington began to look very much like that found in most other settings.

The Peak-McCann bill made it abundantly clear that once the requisite number of signatures had been secured and the petitions were filed with the county clerk, the City Commission and the County Fiscal Court had no choice. They had to appoint a "representative commission composed of not less than twenty citizens."[12]

On the surface, this petitioning procedure seemed to open the way for ordinary citizens to get around the often difficult task of getting local politicians to initiate a move that could ultimately affect their power and status. Certainly KRS 67A provided for more citizen input than Virginia law, which requires the elected officials of the units of government involved both to initiate and to draft a merger charter to be submitted to the voters.[13] It clearly provided more room for citizen initiative than the procedure followed in Nashville, Jacksonville, and many other merger settings, where local officials were simply empowered to appoint such a commission at their discretion.[14] In some respects, the Kentucky law even placed more authority in the hands of local citizens to initiate the merger process than did the Georgia law requiring a local referendum to determine voter sentiment concerning the creation of a charter commission.[15]

There were, however, several basic flaws in the Peak-McCann bill that allowed hostile local officials to thwart the authority vested in the people by the petitioning procedure. KRS 67A did not set a time limit within which local governments had to comply with the legal requirement to appoint a charter commission, once the petitions were filed. And the statute said nothing about how the work of such a commission was to be financed.

It quickly became apparent that the Underwood faction was going to employ the first of these loopholes in the law to stall for time. County Judge Robert Stephens, who had come out publicly in favor of merger during the petition drive, got the Fayette County

Fiscal Court to appoint fifteen citizens to serve on the merger commission shortly after the petitions were filed.[16] But the City Commission refused to act on the matter.

One indication of what was about to happen came three days after the merger petitions were filed with the county clerk. Underwood and his two faithful companions from the City Commission appeared before a state legislative subcommittee to express their views concerning the future status of Lexington. The trio told the legislators that they preferred to have Lexington reclassified as a first-class city, provided that something could be done to allow it to retain the manager form of government.[17] Such a move, of course, would have eliminated any possibility of merger since the Peak-McCann bill specifically exempted counties containing first-class cities from its provisions.

They also told the legislators that they preferred annexation over merger as a way of solving many of the pressing problems of urbanization in the Lexington area. Ironically, this assertion came on the heels of a major decision by the Underwood regime to delay implementation of the massive annexation plan passed by the previous city administration.

Taken together, these two sets of recommendations amounted to an endorsement of the status quo over the implementation of a merger plan. First-class city status would be acceptable only if Lexington would be allowed to retain its present form of government rather than accept the mayor-council form prescribed for first-class cities. In addition, there could be no major alterations in the nature of the city electorate until at least 1975 under the Underwood approach to annexation. With the office of mayor and all seats on the City Commission coming up for grabs in November of 1971, it might be argued that the Underwood faction was fighting to preserve the system under which it had been elected. First-class city status, under the terms offered by Underwood, would only ensure that the disruptive threat of merger could be avoided.

In any event, there was nothing in the comments made by the Underwood forces before the subcommittee to encourage those who had worked so hard to get the merger petition drive completed. This was followed by weeks of total silence from the City Commission on the question of appointing anyone to serve on the merger commission. Even the announcement on December 1, 1970, that the county had complied with the law failed to prompt any action or comment from Underwood.

The silence continued until January 7, 1971, when several members of GO appeared before the regular weekly meeting of the City Commission to request an explanation for the delay. They were met with obvious hostility as Commissioner Underwood publicly attacked various members of GO, who, he felt, were "out to get him." In addition, he expressed the view that merger could be used to take governmental powers "out of the hands of elected officials."[18]

The one positive thing that came out of the confrontation between GO and Commissioner Underwood during that meeting was a statement by the city officials that they were working on a contract to be submitted to the county on the subject. According to Underwood, the contract was necessary in order to specify the relationship between the city and county on the operation of such a commission as well as to establish in writing "who appoints how many members" to such a commission.[19]

On the basis of reports from County Judge Robert Stephens and other sources, it appeared that the major obstacle to the consummation of such a contract was a dispute over the proportion of the commission the city ought to be allowed to appoint. Although the law spoke only of a "representative citizen commission" composed of not fewer than twenty people, the city maintained that it should be allowed to appoint a substantial majority of any commission established, on the grounds that approximately two-thirds of all Fayette County citizens lived in the city. Since the county had already named fifteen members, the Underwood faction argued, surely the city was entitled to name more than that number.

For the next month the county argued that both governing bodies were equal in their authority and responsibility under the law, and that each body should therefore appoint an equal number of members to the commission. Besides, the county argued, if anybody deserved to have a larger number of appointees it was the county. Since it embraced *all* citizens of the community, of which approximately two-thirds were also city residents, the county seemed to deserve a greater share of the total number of seats on the merger commission than the city.

In the end, Underwood accepted the legal interpretation of equality. On February 18, 1971, he finally consented to a contract allowing the city to name fifteen members to the merger commission.[20] Why, after several months of successful delaying tactics, he agreed to such a move remains a mystery. Perhaps it was, as some observers have suggested, simply because Underwood thought that such a commission was only going to study the idea of merger. Perhaps it was because he believed that under the terms of the contract which gave an equal voice to city and county appointees, his fifteen members could stall any real action toward producing a comprehensive plan of urban county government that did not meet with his approval.

Whatever the reasons, Underwood appointed fifteen members to the commission on February 18, 1971.[21] For the most part, the city appointees confirmed the worst fears of the promerger forces in the community. County Judge Robert Stephens, a Democrat, had gotten his Democratic colleagues on the Fiscal Court to go along with appointing eight Democrats and seven Republicans. Among them were representatives from business and labor, blacks and whites, men and women, and city and county residents. When the Underwood list came out, it contained the names of Commissioner Ray Boggs, one of Underwood's staunchest allies on the City Commission; a young pro-Underwood attorney from the city Law Department; Underwood's campaign treasurer; the campaign treasurer's wife (who worked for the Lexington Parks and Recreation Department); and a number of low-level city employees who were thought to be Underwood supporters. In addition, he appointed a county resident who had helped lead the fight against the previous administration's large-scale annexation ordinance. The remainder of his appointees were virtually unknown in civic affairs, although most, if not all of them, were suspected by the proponents of merger of harboring strong pro-Underwood sentiments.

Given the list of Underwood appointees, it was assumed by some county members that an attempt would be made to frustrate the work of the commission from the outset. Although no efforts were made to organize county appointees prior to the first meeting of the entire commission in March 1971, several of them came prepared to force an immediate showdown by introducing a motion that I serve as the temporary chairman of the commission, pending the adoption of formal bylaws to govern its operations. To the surprise of most county appointees, the motion was adopted by a unanimous vote.

Perhaps even more surprisingly, the Underwood appointees quickly endorsed a seemingly fair and reasonable set of bylaws written by a special committee composed of an equal number of city and county appointees. This was followed by the passage of a totally uncontested motion to elect me as the permanent chairman of the group. Neither event squared with the expectations of those who had watched Underwood in action.

Clearly the Underwood people could have tied the commission up in knots during the deliberations over these initial steps. At minimum, they could have created a direct confrontation over the question of leadership by nominating their obvious leader, Commissioner Ray Boggs, to oppose any candidate sponsored by the county delegation. But they chose not to do so.

Some observers again argued that the Underwood appointees did not seize upon these obvious chances to thwart the work of the commission because they fundamentally misunderstood the legal task imposed by the Peak-McCann bill. There may be some merit in this line of argument; many of the city appointees displayed surprise when they were told at the first meeting of the commission that they were required to do more than study the feasibility of such an idea for Lexington and Fayette County.

Others argued that it made little sense for the Underwood forces to push Ray Boggs, or anyone else from their ranks, into competition for the most visible leadership position on the commission. In view of the legal necessity of actually devising a plan or charter for merger to be submitted to the voters, it would have been politically awkward to have an Underwood appointee leading the way. To be sure, Ray Boggs and another Underwood appointee, City Attorney John Daughaday, were elected as vice-chairman and treasurer of the group. (The commission's bylaws specified that the positions of chairman and vice-chairman, as well as the offices of secretary and treasurer, had to be shared equally among city and county appointees.) But neither of the offices held by Boggs and Daughaday carried much visibility. As far as the press was concerned, it was the chairman who was to attract most of the praise or blame for what went on during the meetings of the commission.

But there were more subtle tactics available to the Underwood appointees to harass the work of the commission. While the evidence does not support the contentions by some observers that the city appointees engaged in a conspiracy to do so, several things began to happen shortly after the commission had adopted its bylaws and elected its permanent officers. Attendance by city appointees began to fall off dramatically, making it more and more difficult for the commission to obtain a quorum. Executive committee meetings were constantly tied up in debates over trivial and often irrelevant points raised by Boggs and some of his fellow city appointees. And there were constant pleas from certain Underwood appointees not to proceed too swiftly with writing the comprehensive plan for merging the city and county governments.

While bothersome, these tactics did not bring the work of the commission to a complete standstill. In fact, several city appointees, including Underwood's former campaign treasurer and the attorney from the city Law Department, began to show genuine enthusiasm for the merger idea. Further cracks in the solidarity of the city appointees seemed to appear in August 1971 when the results of a poll paid for by the city (at Underwood's request) showed substantial support for the merger idea among city voters.[22] Finally, it became obvious that the city appointees to the commission found it increasingly difficult to act as a bloc. It is one thing for a political faction to secure the obedience of appointees in a nominating convention, for instance, where the choice is between candidates A and B. But when a group is dealing with complex questions about the contents of a charter, it becomes exceedingly difficult for a coalition of political amateurs to operate effectively. Unless members are allowed to caucus at every twist and turn of events, such a group begins to fall apart.

Low attendance among city-appointed members was a persistent problem. Some county appointees were also at fault when it came to producing quorums, but the Fayette County Fiscal Court tended to follow the terms of the bylaws adopted by the commission, which called upon the original appointing authority to replace any member who resigned or who missed three consecutive regular meetings of the commission. The city administration, on the other hand, seemed content to tolerate noncompliance with the attendance rules. Nine of the fifteen city appointees, for example, were cited for chronic nonattendance during the period between July and December of 1971. Yet only three of these were replaced by the Underwood administration. Since unfilled vacancies and chronic nonattendance reduced the pool from which a quorum of sixteen had to be drawn, the actions of the Underwood majority on the City Commission proved to be quite frustrating. In the period June–December 1971, three of the monthly meetings failed to attract a quorum, and at a fourth meeting only the bare quorum was present.

One of the most serious problems facing the charter commission during the Underwood era, however, was money. The city and county governments had agreed in March 1971 to put up an initial sum of $300 apiece to purchase stationery and other supplies. In addition, the city offered a small, single-room office in a city-owned building used by the City-County Planning Commission and the City-County Human Rights Commission. The Fayette County Fiscal Court agreed to supply some surplus and very well used office equipment.

After several months of begging by the commission, it was announced that the city would appropriate $6,500 to the merger commission for the fiscal year beginning on July 1, 1971. The Fayette County Fiscal Court, which operated on a relatively smaller fiscal base, agreed to match that sum.

A total sum of $13,600, plus the services in kind promised by the city and county, seemed almost impressive at the time. It allowed the merger commission to purchase needed supplies, install a telephone, purchase a number of documents and charters from other merger settings, and hire a full-time "secretary–research assistant."

There were, however, no funds for outside consulting firms or an executive director to coordinate the work of the commission. Even more disturbing was the fact that by the fall of 1971 the city began to neglect its monthly payment of approximately $550 under the terms of the appropriation ordinance. Soon the commission was forced to pay its bills—for salaries, supplies, telephone, and so on —out of the $550 supplied by the county each month. By the end of the year, the city was five months behind in its payments and the commission was on the verge of financial ruin.

Two alternatives seemed open to the commission: to appeal to the county to take up the slack, or to solicit support from private interests. But there was little chance that the former would work and the latter involved major risks.

Serious fiscal and political considerations prevented the Fayette County Fiscal Court from helping out. On the one hand, the county operated on a relatively limited budget. Its total tax resources were only a fraction of the city's. Furthermore, the county had agreed to the proposition of equality in staffing and funding under a contract that had been insisted upon by the city. To have agreed to cover the city's deficits in funding the commission would have been tantamount to breaking this contract—and it would have been politically insane in view of the growing public disenchantment with the general fiscal irresponsibility of the Underwood regime.

Turning to private supporters seemed attractive to a number of merger commission members during the early stages of the city's financial boycott. But this would have meant turning to precisely those kinds of groups in the community that are often cited by the opponents of merger when they argue that city-county consolidation is an elitist, business-oriented plot against the common citizens. More important, the persistent evidence that the city meant to renege on its obligations to the commission did not begin to become obvious until after the municipal primaries were held in September of 1971. Although Underwood had been eliminated from the race for mayor in that primary, three members of his slate had succeeded in getting into the City Commission race that would be decided in the general election in November. This meant that those individuals and groups most interested in the cause of merger were primarily committed to the defeat of the residue of Underwood supporters left in the race. It seemed unlikely that any substantial private resources could be tapped by the merger commission in such a situation.

The Lexington-Fayette County Merger Commission was therefore obliged to await the outcome of the 1971 general election in the hope that a more responsive and sympathetic city administration would take over in January 1972. Either of the remaining candidates for mayor would have been more sympathetic to the work of the commission than the eliminated Underwood, although Foster Pettit seemed more openly and genuinely committed to the idea than his opponent, former City Commissioner Harry Sykes. The race for control of the City Commission, however, pitted the three Underwood supporters who had survived the primary against a Pettit slate and Edgar Wallace, who was running as an independent.

With Underwood eliminated from the race during the September primary, Pettit easily won out over the token opposition offered by Sykes. The only real threat to a complete sweep for the Pettit slate was Wallace, who came in a very close fifth in the four-way race for seats on the City Commission. It was a bitter blow for local blacks who had cast a highly disciplined "one-shot" vote for Wallace to succeed Sykes as the only black member on the at-large commission. And it was a lesson in the biases of at-large elections that the leaders of the black community were not to forget.

From the perspective of the merger commission, the most important news was that the Underwood faction had been swept from power. Some might have preferred to see Wallace—a member of GO and secretary of the merger commission—win a seat on the City Commission. But Pettit and his team had swept the field and they had openly endorsed merger during the 1971 municipal elections.

The Pettit forces demonstrated their commitment to the cause by meeting with representatives of the merger commission shortly after the November election. By the time the Pettit administration took office in January 1972 it had agreed that (a) the city would pay all of the monthly allotments to the commission left over from the Underwood era, and (b) the city would appropriate an additional $5,000 above and beyond the financial commitment they inherited from the Underwood administration for the remaining six months in the fiscal year. This additional $5,000 was matched by the Fayette County Fiscal Court. These additional sums were to be used to hire more staff and to allow the chairman of the merger commission to take a part-time leave from the University of Kentucky for the period January through June in order to spend more time on the merger project.

Services in kind to the commission were also increased after January 1, 1972. The city renovated part of the building that housed the commission office, making available a three-room suite of offices and space for committee meetings. (The full commission met on the University of Kentucky campus.) The county furnished the new offices and supplied additional office equipment. The new space and equipment were functional (though hardly plush) and very badly needed.

With the financial crisis out of the way, Mayor Pettit tackled the problem of replacing ten city appointees to the commission who had either resigned or demonstrated a pattern of chronic non-attendance.[23]

The first batch of new appointees, five in number, included Dr. Malcolm Jewell from the Department of Political Science at the University of Kentucky, a nationally known scholar of legislative bodies and legislative reapportionment; William McCann, one of the cosponsors of the state enabling legislation under which the commission operated; and Marian Jordan, a leader in GO during the petition drive and an active member of the League of Women Voters; the executive director of the local American Red Cross, who had persistently expressed an interest in becoming a member of the group; and John Butler, Jr., a very articulate black man who was in the personnel department of IBM.

The second batch of appointments seemed to be more political in nature. Most of the appointees in this group seemed to have very definite and obvious interests to protect. City Commissioner J. Farra Van Meter, for example, the leading vote-getter on the Pettit team, was included in this second wave of appointments, as were the mayor's secretary, a ranking officer from the city police department, and an officer from the city fire department.

Clearly the 1971 municipal election marked a major turning point in the history of the merger movement in Lexington. It is exceedingly doubtful that the Lexington-Fayette County Merger Commission would ever have completed its task had it not been for the defeat of the Underwood forces in 1971 and the positive support given to the commission by the newly elected Pettit administration. Without the financial support generated by the city and county, the charter commission would have been in serious trouble. And without the infusion of new blood ordered by the new city administration, the commission would have had to limp along trying to get enough people to hold meetings.

Perhaps the greatest lesson to be drawn from the Lexington experience up to this point is that, regardless of how the enabling legislation is drawn, it is very difficult for the proponents of city-county consolidation to initiate consolidation efforts without at least a modicum of support from local political incumbents. In the Lexington case state law seemed to ensure that city and county officials would create a charter commission upon the petition of ordinary citizens. Yet despite this atypical legal feature, the events in Lexington demonstrated the extremely vulnerable position of a charter commission established in the face of the objections and hostile attitudes of a powerful group of political officeholders.[24]

Equally important, however, is the fact that, once the Underwood faction was removed from the scene by the voters, the project moved forward with ease. Attendance at commission meetings shot upward, the executive committee began to pour out proposals for the full commission to consider, and supporters of the project began to take heart again. On June 20, 1972, less than six months after the Pettit regime took over in the city, the charter was finished.

Many hours were devoted to the project in those last few months —more than had been spent during the entire ten months in the life of the commission preceding the installation of the Pettit administration in January of 1972. The commission met regularly every month. Its executive committee met at least once a week, often until eleven or twelve o'clock at night. And its staff often put in hours that would make wage-and-hour law overseers cringe.

It was not enough that the county judge and the members of the Fayette County Fiscal Court had leaped to the aid of the merger project from the outset, although their support during the petition drive and the first ten months of the commission's existence should not be forgotten. The crucial difference came after the defeat of the uncooperative Underwood faction in the city. The balance of power had shifted so that both city and county governments were now committed to the merger project.

5

The Underwood Era

EVERY CITY-COUNTY consolidation campaign is ultimately mounted and fought over a plan or charter for establishing a merged government in a particular community. Admittedly, very few voters ever read these charters, and voter knowledge of their contents tends to be quite limited.[1] However, important groups in the community often support or oppose merger on the basis of how a particular charter treats, or is perceived to treat, such matters as taxation, representation, or the procedures for expanding urban services into new areas. As one observer put it, "Success at the polls demands a reorganization proposal . . . that will permit all major groups involved to gain, or to think they will gain, from the change."[2]

Given the importance attached to these charters, it is frustrating to discover that little is known about their actual drafting. We know that the boards or commissions that draft these documents generally have considerable legal latitude in deciding how a proposed consolidated government is to be structured. It is even possible to compare and contrast the basic features of the various charters that have been submitted to local electorates over the years. But it has been exceedingly difficult to obtain hard information about how charter commissions arrive at the myriad decisions that go into the preparation of these charters.

It is important, therefore, that we examine the drafting of the Lexington charter on the basis of the records and tape recordings of the meetings held by the Lexington-Fayette County Merger Commission and its executive committee. Although it will not be possible to make detailed comparisons based on similar information about the work of other charter commissions, we can at least document how the Lexington commission went about the task of preparing a quite typical merger document.

One of the purposes of having a "representative citizen commission" devise a merger charter is to help ensure that such a document reflects the views of various segments of the community. But it is clear that multimember boards and commissions generally find it difficult to collectively perform every step in the process of producing complex decisions.

Although the basic dimensions of this problem were understood from the outset, the chairman of the Lexington commission attempted to follow the well-worn path of instituting a system of specialized standing committees shortly after the group was organized in the spring of 1971. Ten rather small committees were to conduct studies concerning various aspects of merging the city and county governments.[3] In addition, it was hoped that each of these smaller groups would be able to generate specific proposals to be considered for inclusion in a proposed plan or charter. An executive committee, composed of the four elected officers of the commission and the chairperson of each of the ten standing committees, was established to coordinate the activities of the various groups and resolve whatever conflicts might arise before proposals were sent to the full commission.

For the most part, the strategy behind the creation of this committee system was unsuccessful. The committee on health and welfare eventually submitted a well-documented report of how these functions were performed under the existing system, as well as a set of recommendations concerning the performance of these functions under merger. Near the end of the commission's deliberations, the committee on the judiciary met and made several recommendations, but only in direct response to specific questions put forward by the chairman and the executive committee. The committee on government organization, which had been assigned perhaps the most central and overarching responsibilities within the whole standing committee system, performed well. However, it operated almost exclusively in joint meetings with the executive committee. As a group, it generated few proposals and acted primarily as a vehicle to help expand the numerical base upon which executive committee deliberations and recommendations were premised.

Beyond these noteworthy exceptions, the standing committee idea was a complete failure. Perhaps much of the blame can be attributed to the general decline in morale and enthusiasm that swept over the work of the commission during the "Underwood era." Perhaps it was because the chairman of the commission eventually established a procedural format that simply circumvented the standing committees during that period. Once established, this modus operandi was difficult to change.

In retrospect, however, it may have been naïve for anyone to expect ten rather specialized committees, composed of citizens who could not devote full time to the task, to conduct research and formulate proposals. A merger charter is a complex document composed of numerous interrelated parts. It must be based on sophisticated research, framed in tightly worded legal language, and subjected to technical scrutiny. These are difficult tasks for most groups of laymen.

Whatever the reasons, it had become evident by August 1971 that the committee system was not working in the Lexington setting. Many ideas concerning basic policy had been discussed, but little was being done to formulate proposals for the commission to consider. It was essential that someone pull these ideas together, translate them into specific proposals, submit them to the executive committee, revise them if necessary, and prepare something to be placed before the full commission for debate.

Some charter commissions have hired private consulting firms or full-time executive directors to perform many of these research and drafting tasks. Since the Lexington commission was in no financial position to adopt this idea, the chairman decided in August 1971 to assume the task of preparing a set of proposals to be submitted to the commission. The initial set of proposals prepared under this arrangement concerned several general policy options that had been discussed and even subjected to a series of "straw votes" during the summer of 1971.

Although the proposals prepared for the September 1971 meeting were considerably more detailed and complete than anything the commission had dealt with previously, they were not stated in formal charter language, and thus they could not be given first reading under the terms of the commission's bylaws. The best that could be done was to schedule a debate on the proposals and hope to adopt motions to have them worked into final legal language and resubmitted for first reading.

While this procedure got the commission to begin thinking about translating ideas into concrete proposals, it promised to be time-consuming. At minimum, it would take three months to adopt a section of the proposed charter: one monthly meeting to debate and vote on proposals to be reworked into final legal language; another to give first reading to the reworked proposal; and, since the bylaws required that any item given first reading lie over at least one month, yet another monthly meeting for formal adoption.[4]

In view of this, the chairman issued an executive order at the October 1971 meeting to change the procedural format. Henceforth, all items submitted to the commission for possible inclusion in the charter would be stated in the proper legal form for giving the matter first reading. In addition, weekly meetings of the executive committee were instituted to review the work of all standing committees, discuss policy proposals, and approve all items to be submitted to the full commission for first reading.

In practice, these procedural guidelines evolved into a system in which the chairman acted as the executive director of the commission. Virtually all needed research was done under his direction. He supervised the staff of the commission, which was expanded to three full-time people at the start of the "Pettit era." Finally, he set the agenda for the executive committee and the full commission and was responsible for drafting all proposals submitted to these groups.

This is not to suggest that either the executive committee or the full commission was reduced to the status of merely legitimizing the work of the chairman and his staff. The tape recordings of the meetings of both bodies, and the newspaper accounts of many of these meetings simply will not support such a conclusion. Both bodies conducted vigorous debates and suggested many changes, large and small, concerning the proposals placed before them. Indeed the executive committee, particularly during the "Pettit era," proved singularly adept at hammering out sound proposals to be submitted to the commission on the basis of ideas and recommendations made by the chairman and his staff.

One other point ought to be made about the way the Lexington commission operated. It was decided very early to hold all meetings of the commission and its executive committee open to the public and to encourage the press to attend. This was a crucial decision, not so much from the standpoint of actually getting large numbers of citizens to attend commission meetings, but in making it clear that what was being done was open to public scrutiny.

The problem of organizing and administering the work of the charter commission was not the only thing that stood in the way of moving forward with the task at hand during the Underwood era. The Peak-McCann bill left much to the imagination in defining the scope of the charter commission's authority. Although the bill charged such commissions with "devising a comprehensive plan of urban county government," it failed to mention what was to be included in such a plan.[5] As a result, it left open the question of how far a commission could go toward altering or abolishing various city and county offices in order to achieve merger, or what alternatives were open to such commissions in prescribing the organization and structure of an urban county government.

Sections of KRS 67A concerning the powers and duties of an "urban county government" gave little clarification. The statute did say that an urban county government would have all of the "powers and privileges possessed by the class of cities to which the largest city in the county belonged on June 19, 1970."[6] But that left the question of what was going to happen to a number of important functions (courts, welfare systems, and maintenance of rural roads, for example) that were performed by the existing county but not by cities of the second class. Similarly, the provision in the bill that "all debts, property, franchises, and rights of any municipality within the county shall be assumed by the urban county government" merely raised the question of what was to be done with the debts and obligations of the existing county government, which were entirely separate from those incurred by cities.[7]

A second problem was that the law discussed only the powers and obligations of an urban county government. Did the term *powers* embrace the notion of organization and structure? In conferring the powers of a second-class city upon an urban county government, did the Peak-McCann bill also call for the adoption of the form and structure found in the city of Lexington at the time the charter was written? If so, what was to be done with the many county officers prescribed for all counties by the state constitution (county judge, clerk, jailer, sheriff, assessor, and so forth)? Or did the law mean that an urban county government would be little more than a county government with additional legal powers, and that therefore the existing organization and structure of Fayette County would have to be maintained?

No one, it appeared, was prepared to argue that an urban county government was supposed to be merely a county with the additional powers of a second-class city, or that an urban county government would have to be headed by a county fiscal court and county judge. There were, however, those who argued that KRS 67A spoke only of the powers and obligations of second-class cities. Their plea was to treat the enabling legislation under which the commission operated as essentially a statement of what could be done within the confines of existing statutes and constitutional provisions governing cities of that class.

This line of argument was never articulated as a full-blown legal philosophy, but it was inserted into the deliberations of the commission at various points. It was the basis of the argument that it would be illegal to tamper with the manager form of government employed in the city of Lexington on the grounds that an urban county government could possess only the powers and privileges of the largest city in the county. In this case, the argument continued, an urban county government could have only the powers and privileges of a second-class city organized under existing statutes governing a second-class city with a manager form of government, or what passed for the manager form in Kentucky.

This same line of argument was also used to resist the idea of granting veto powers to the chief executive of the new government. It figured in discussions of the future status of various independent boards and commissions operating in the city of Lexington. Finally, it was invoked during the debate over whether the merger commission could abandon the at-large system of representation used in Lexington in favor of a single-member district plan.

Given the restrictions placed upon the commission by those who wanted to fit the concept of an urban county government into the constitutional and statutory mold prescribed for a second-class city, it came as no surprise that some members of the Lexington-Fayette County Merger Commission began to argue for a more liberal interpretation of the Peak-McCann bill. The most persistent and outspoken advocate of a more liberal interpretation was Rufus Lisle, a prominent attorney who had been appointed to the commission by the County Fiscal Court.

Reduced to its basic features, the position taken by Lisle was that KRS 67A gave the commission a broad grant of authority to restructure local government in the community. Granting the commission the power to "devise a comprehensive plan," he argued, was tantamount to granting home rule to the community. In addition, Lisle asserted that the law called for the creation of a totally new entity to be known as an urban county government. This new entity, he concluded, would be neither a county nor a city—it would be both.

It was Lisle's contention, therefore, that the commission should not quibble over what the statutes said about such things as the executive powers of county judges or mayors of second-class cities. If the merger commission wanted to strip the county judge of his statutory administrative powers or give the chief executive of the new government veto power, it could do so on the grounds that none of the existing statutes applied to urban county governments. The same theme ran through his arguments on district representation, civil service reform, structure of executive departments, and the abolition of certain independent boards and commissions.

Although the Lexington-Fayette County Merger Commission ultimately adopted the essential features of this liberal interpretation, there was sufficient concern over the legal risks involved to prompt the commission to press the 1972 session of the General Assembly to amend KRS 67A. One amendment sought to clarify the meaning of the term "comprehensive plan." As a result of the pleas of Mayor Foster Pettit, County Judge Robert Stephens, and the chairman of the merger commission to the House Committee on Cities, section .020 of the statute was amended to read as follows: "The plan shall include a description of the form, structure, functions, powers and officers and the duties of the proposed urban county government; the procedures by which the original plan may be amended; and such other provisions as the commission shall determine."

The problem of disposing of the powers and obligations of the existing county government was handled as follows: section .030 of the statute was amended to read: "All debts, property, franchises and rights of *the existing county government and of* any municipality within the county shall be assumed by the urban county government" (amendment in italics). In addition, section .040 was amended to include the following: "All powers and privileges possessed by *the County and* by the class of cities to which the largest city in the county belongs *on the date the urban county government becomes the effective government* shall be exercised by the urban county government" (amendment in italics).

Although these amendments helped to soothe some of the concerns expressed by those who basically sided with the Rufus Lisle interpretation of the Peak-McCann legislation, they failed to answer the question of how far the commission ought to push its legal mandate. For example, some of those who seemed prepared to endorse a liberal interpretation of KRS 67A when it came to a total restructuring of such things as the system of representation would often question the wisdom of pushing the commission's luck by flouting existing legal practices and requirements concerning the status of independent airport boards, library boards, or public housing authorities.

Gradually a tacit policy was developed that allowed the commission to construe KRS 67A very broadly when it was deemed absolutely necessary to do so. Time and time again, as we shall see, the commission struck an innovative chord on basic policy questions. But it also refused to expose the charter to any more legal challenges than seemed necessary to satisfy strong public sentiments or deep-seated convictions on the part of a solid majority of its members. In short, the commission opted for a modified version of the Rufus Lisle position even though it had argued for and won several amendments to the Peak-McCann legislation that clearly strengthened the legal vitality of that position.

Several months went by before the Lexington commission began discussing any of the substantive issues surrounding the problem of devising a comprehensive plan. Its first meeting, on March 16, 1971, was spent electing temporary officers and creating an ad hoc committee to draw up a set of bylaws. The March 30 and April meetings were devoted to adopting the bylaws and electing permanent officers.

During the May meeting the commission reviewed the concept of city-county consolidation and discussed some of the basic features of other merger charters. But this was purely an exploratory educational experience for most of those present and did not result in any debate on what ought to be included in a comprehensive plan for merging the city and county governments in the Lexington community.

It was in this same spirit of exploring ideas that the commission scheduled a special meeting on June 1 to hear the views of various community groups on such basic questions as: Which form of government would be best for the Lexington community—the Mayor-Council or the Council-Manager form? Would it be better to have partisan or nonpartisan elections for local offices? What system of representation is best at the local level—strictly at-large, single-member districts only, or some combination thereof?

Despite several public notices in the local press and written invitations to more than two dozen community organizations, spokesmen for only six local groups attended the June 1 meeting. This was the first clue the commission received that it would be difficult to get widespread community participation in the formulation of a charter. Nevertheless, the commission did receive written or oral testimony from GO, CORE, Omega Psi Phi (a local black fraternity), the Lexington-Fayette County Human Rights Commission, the local League of Women Voters, and the Greater Lexington Chamber of Commerce.

Perhaps the most important outcome of the special meeting was the discovery that none of these groups wanted to preserve the existing structural arrangements of either the city or the county government. Moreover, there was considerable agreement among these groups about the kind of structural package they would prefer. Most of the groups, for example, urged the commission to provide for a strong elected chief executive if at all possible. The manager idea, or at least the flaccid version of that idea available under existing state laws, was rejected as inadequate by everyone who testified except Robert Jefferson, who spoke for several black groups. The concern of blacks, he said, was that a "strong mayor might lead to political bossism."[8] Similarly, all but one of these groups endorsed the idea of nonpartisan elections. Only GO supported partisan elections. But it did so more in the interest of keeping the idea alive for future consideration than out of any strong commitment to fight for its inclusion in the charter.[9]

On the question of representation alone were there significant differences of opinion. Several groups, including GO, the Chamber of Commerce, and the League of Women Voters, leaned toward a legislative body composed of some at-large members and some district representatives, though they differed somewhat when it came to specifying what proportion of the council ought to be elected from districts.[10] Other groups, particularly those representing blacks, pressed the idea of having only district representation. Either way the basic message was the same—get rid of the exclusively at-large representation then employed in both the city and county.

On the basis of what these groups had said, it seemed important for the commission to begin probing its own stand on these basic questions. It was therefore decided that, beginning with the regular monthly meeting scheduled for June 15, 1971, the commission would discuss each of these policy options. It was further decided that a "straw vote" would be conducted among those present after the discussion on each question. This would allow the commission to ascertain the basic thrust of sentiment among its members without having to formally invoke the provision in the bylaws calling for sixteen members to endorse any provision that was to become part of the comprehensive plan.

The first item on the agenda for the June 15 meeting was the question of representation. Four separate motions were made that included references to single-member district representation. One called for a system of representation based on districts only. One called for a combination of district and at-large representation. Another suggested that some members of the urban county legislative body be elected from rather small districts and some from larger geographical areas or zones. There was also a proposal to have some members elected from single-member districts, and a few members elected at large but required to reside in defined areas or zones. Although they varied considerably in detail, each of these proposals was premised on the assumption that the commission was free to alter the exclusively at-large systems employed in both the city and county.[11]

Two other ideas concerning representation were also presented that night. One of these was that all members of the legislative body ought to be elected by the voters at large. This, of course, was the system used in the city of Lexington. The other endorsed the essential features of the system used in the county, where members of the Fiscal Court were elected at large, but had to reside in designated areas or districts.

Seventeen of the twenty members present supported proposals that contained references to single-member districts, though there was little agreement on details. The number of district-oriented proposals had been reduced from four to three when the complicated plan calling for district plus zone representatives failed to attract any support in the straw vote. With only two members supporting the district-only proposal, it was also clear that sentiment ran heavily in favor of some kind of combined district/at-large proposal. The problem was that the supporters of such a combination split almost evenly between those who would require the at-large members to reside in zones (eight votes) and those who did not favor the residence requirement (seven votes).

The only other straw vote taken during the regular June meeting concerned the question of partisan versus nonpartisan elections. Although eighteen of the twenty members present supported the latter, the vote did not involve any direct confrontation over the scope and meaning of the Peak-McCann bill.[12] There were only two choices available and both were currently employed in the community (partisan elections in the county, nonpartisan in the city).

A confrontation over the meaning of the Peak-McCann bill did arise at the next meeting of the commission, on July 20, 1971. And this time the lines were openly and candidly drawn as Rufus Lisle and City Commissioner Ray Boggs began the debate over what type of executive the new government ought to have. Commissioner Boggs argued that the merger commission had to choose between the elected county judge system used in the county and the manager form employed in the city. As expected, Rufus Lisle maintained that the commission was not bound by these precedents, and that it ought to "come up with a plan that is best for the community," without trying to "make the proposal fit into existing law."[13]

As the debate shifted to more substantive matters, it became increasingly evident that there was substantial agreement among those present on several basic points. First, no one wanted to build the office of chief executive around the existing institution of county judge. Although the Fayette County judge had come to resemble the strong elected chief executive advocated by many, it was generally understood that this had been the result of factors other than the legal powers vested in the office. It was primarily the personal leadership and political power of Judge Robert Stephens and several of his predecessors which had left their mark on the office and not simply the statutes pertaining to their executive authority.

The second point on which there seemed to be a general consensus was that the city manager form of government as spelled out in existing state laws was less than adequate. This led some commission members to reject the manager idea out of hand. Others wondered if it might not be possible to provide for a more adequate council-manager system in the charter. Finally, there were those who wondered if it would not be possible to inject some element of professionalism into the executive office of the new government by providing a strong, elected chief executive with some sort of administrative assistant who would have the qualifications generally thought of when the term city manager is mentioned.

This last idea seemed to capture the imagination of most of those attending the July meeting. But the leading spokesmen for the idea were pressing for something more than simply providing an elected chief executive with an administrative assistant along the lines suggested by the Jacksonville charter. They seemed to be advocating a *strong* elected mayor, along with a reasonably independent professional administrative assistant with sufficient authority to direct the attention of the urban county council toward professional considerations in such areas as personnel, budgeting, and general executive management.[14]

How this was to be spelled out in the charter was not made entirely clear, but the outline presented by Eric Karnes and Edgar Wallace seemed to prepare the way for a coalition between those who wanted a strong elected chief executive, and those who clung to the council-manager idea despite the legal limitations imposed upon city managers under existing state laws. However, only fourteen members were in attendance at the July meeting, and with two members abstaining on the question, the straw vote on the Karnes-Wallace idea fell four votes short of the sixteen that would eventually be required to have it included in the proposed charter.[15]

Nothing more was done on the subject of establishing the basic form and structure of the proposed merged government until September. (Since only fifteen members attended the August meeting, it was impossible to move forward with the ideas tested in the straw votes conducted at the two previous monthly meetings.) With a reassuring twenty-one members present at the September meeting, the commission took up a series of specific proposals prepared by the chairman based on the straw vote results. After some spirited debate, the commission went on record in favor of:

(a) A fifteen-member urban county council composed of twelve members elected from single-member districts, and three elected at large

(b) Two-year terms for district council members and four-year terms for at-large members

(c) Compensation for all council members set at $6,000 per year (the same as city commissioners were then getting)

(d) A limit of four consecutive terms for district members and two for at-large members

(e) Election of all council members on a nonpartisan ballot

(f) A requirement that all members of the council must have resided within the territory governed by the merged government for at least one year before filing as a candidate, with an additional six-month residence within their district required of all district candidates

(g) The creation and periodic redistricting of all council districts by the council on the basis of population equality, and within that framework such additional criteria as "community or diversity of interests," "relative rates of growth," and "patterns of social and economic interests."[16]

Two other proposals were returned to the executive committee for more work. One of these concerned the method of selecting a vice-mayor. Some commission members wanted the vice-mayor to be selected by the council from the three at-large members. Others sought to have the office filled by a vote of the council from its entire membership. And some wanted to designate the at-large member who had obtained the highest number of votes in the most recent general election for at-large seats. The other item resubmitted concerned filling vacancies on the council. The dispute was over holding special elections versus allowing the chief executive to fill vacancies by appointment.

All the proposals approved that night were quickly worked into final legal language and approved by the executive committee to be submitted to the full commission for second reading. Despite decreasing attendance, the executive committee also plunged ahead with the idea that the vice-mayor should be selected by the council from the three at-large members. On the question of filling vacancies, the executive committee opted for a compromise solution. It endorsed the idea of allowing the mayor to fill vacancies if less than half a term was at stake; otherwise a special election would be called.

All these proposals were put in final form and circulated among the full commission membership before the October meeting, when second reading was scheduled for these sections of what was to become article 4 of the proposed charter. Unfortunately, only fifteen members were in their seats when the meeting was called to order—one short of a quorum. With that, the commission resolved itself into a committee of the whole to conduct a much-needed discussion with City Manager Edgar Maroney about the problems inherent in state law concerning the operation of the city-manager form of government in Kentucky.[17]

Twenty-three members attended the November 16 meeting of the commission. After more than an hour of debate, most of it centering on the proposals concerning the selection of the vice-mayor and the filling of vacancies on the council, the commission managed to give second reading to all of the sections of article 4 that had been cleared for second reading in September. Two other matters were on the agenda that night. One was first reading of a brief and totally uncontentious draft of article 1 dealing with the name and territorial limits of the proposed merged government. The other was a draft proposal concerning taxing and service districts. It too was scheduled for first reading.

As expected, first reading was quickly given to the proposed article 1. The tax-service proposal, however, was a different matter. Commission members and spectators alike began to ask questions about its contents. Because of the complexity of the whole question of taxing and service districts under merger, the chairman waived the rules governing first reading to allow members to raise questions about the meaning and intent of various sections of the proposal.

The third Tuesday in December of 1971 was not an ideal time for a meeting. It was only four days before Christmas, and people could easily excuse themselves from attending a merger commission meeting. In any case, only fifteen members, ten county and five city appointees, answered the roll after a full forty-five-minute delay beyond the scheduled 7:30 P.M. starting time. Although another county appointee arrived by 8:30 to allow a quorum to be called, an hour of precious meeting time had been wasted. Furthermore, it was obvious to everyone present, including the fourteen adult visitors and six members of Boy Scout Troop 95 (who were there to work on their civics merit badge), that any action taken by the commission that night would require unanimous votes.

Article 1, specifying the name and the territorial limits of the proposed urban county government, was given second reading and passed unanimously. In addition, the commission began a debate on several proposals concerning the complicated question of establishing taxing and services districts. Although some progress was made on this last item, the hour soon became late and weary commission members began to press for adjournment.

For those who measured the commission's progress in terms of how many articles or sections of the proposed charter had been completed, there was little to cheer about as the "Underwood era" drew to a close. After ten months of work, the commission had completed a brief article dealing with the name and territorial limits of the proposed merged government, along with several equally uncontentious sections of the article concerning the creation of taxing and services districts which will be discussed later. The only bright spot was the fact that most of article 4 on the proposed council had been put to bed.

This left a tremendous amount of work to be done. The commission had not even started to consider such matters as budget and financial procedures, personnel and pension systems, the urban county courts, amending the charter, or how the transition from the old to the new system of government was to be handled. Nothing had been done about defining the powers and functions of an urban county government, structuring the various executive departments, or deciding what to do about the various independent boards and commissions operating in the community.

Yet it must be noted that, in addition to completing an admittedly tiny fraction of what would have to be included in a proposed plan or charter, the commission had managed to explore a number of fundamental questions concerning the basic form and structure of the proposed urban county government. In addition to completing most sections of an article dealing with the creation of an urban county council that would feature the principles of nonpartisan elections and an emphasis upon district representation, the commission had gone on record in favor of a strong mayor-council system that would also employ an independent professional administrative assistant. In fact, the executive committee had completed most of a draft of article 5 dealing with the office of chief executive, which would be submitted to the commission in January 1972 for first reading. The commission and its executive committee had also explored many of the problems associated with creating and operating a system of different services and taxing districts within the territorial limits of the proposed urban county government.

But could the commission pick up the pace and complete a plan or charter in time to have the question of its adoption placed on the ballot for the 1972 general election scheduled for November 7 of that year? To do so would mean completing the plan or charter by no later than August 2, 1972 in order to comply with the requirement that the plan be advertised at least ninety days before the voters were asked to approve or disapprove its adoption.[18]

It was important that the matter be placed before the electorate in November of 1972. Although KRS 67A did not impose a time limit on the life of the commission, it did specify that the plan or charter, if adopted, could be implemented only "upon the election and qualification of county officers at the *next* regularly scheduled election at which county officers shall be elected" (emphasis added).[19]

Thus if the voters approved a merger plan in November of 1972, it could become effective in January of 1974, following the election and qualification of county officers scheduled by law for November of 1973. But if the plan or charter was placed before the electorate in November of 1973, it could not be implemented until January 1978—that is, following the *next* scheduled election of county officers in November of 1977.

Citing the conventional wisdom that high voter turnout generally attracts a larger proportion of poorly qualified voters to the polls, some argued that such a delay would be useful simply because it might be dangerous to place the question on the ballot during a presidential election, when voter turnout would be high. Others, including the chairman of the commission, argued that the risks of delaying the vote beyond November of 1972 were very great. It would be difficult to sustain public interest in a project over such a long period of time. (Almost three years would have elapsed between the much publicized petition drive in the summer of 1970 to get a commission established and the ninety-day deadline prior to the 1973 general election.) Besides, there seemed to be little systematic empirical evidence that voter turnout had much to do with success or failure at the polls.[20]

By the time the Underwood era drew to a close, most of the active members of the commission had apparently accepted the importance of meeting the August 1972 deadline. Their major concern seemed to be whether the commission could meet the task at hand. To do so, it would have to achieve quorums at every meeting, receive greater and more sustained financial support to hire the kind of staff that could assist in the difficult task of preparing proposals for the commission to consider, and develop the kind of morale that would result in the active participation of virtually every member of the commission. It was on these points that the commission had suffered its greatest blows during the Underwood era. And it was on these points that the success of the commission would rest as it moved into the Pettit era.

6

The Pettit Era

THE NEWLY elected Pettit administration assumed office on January 4, 1972. By January 18, when the merger commission held its next regular monthly meeting, the new regime at city hall had paid all debts to the commission left over from the previous administration, completed an agreement with Fayette County Fiscal Court to supply additional funds to expand the staff of the commission, and replaced five city appointees to the commission who had resigned or been cited for chronic nonattendance. Five more city appointees were replaced before the February meeting of the commission.

It is easy to look back on the Pettit era and observe the very positive impact that the infusion of new people and additional resources had upon the morale and ultimate performance of the merger commission. At the time, however, there was considerable apprehension over whether these efforts to revitalize the commission might also prevent it from completing the charter in time to submit it to the voters in November 1972.

Several members of the commission, for example, expressed their concern that such a large group of new appointees might challenge the basic structural package already worked out. Pointing out that a number of proposals concerning the election, tenure, and powers of the urban county mayor had been hammered out by the executive committee and were scheduled for first reading at the January 1972 meeting of the full commission, they wanted to know whether "Pettit's replacements" would demand a complete rethinking of the strong mayor-council concept that had been endorsed previously.

Some even suggested that those parts of article 4 dealing with the structure of the proposed council that had already been adopted might also be open to attack. The sections covering the criteria for defining council districts and the procedures for handling future redistricting, it was noted, were scheduled for second reading at the January meeting. Not only would this provide an opportunity to reopen the whole question of district versus at-large representation, there would be more than enough opportunities to do so when the commission got around to considering several technical changes being recommended to clarify and polish the language of those sections that already had been given second reading.

The chairman promised that the new appointees would be given a thorough briefing on the previous work of the commission, including the results of the public hearing held on June 1, 1971, and of the subsequent straw votes by the commission that had led to the proposals contained in articles 4 and 5. If this, coupled with being given access to all minutes and tape recordings of the meetings held by the commission and its executive committee, could not persuade these new members to support the basic bargains that had been struck in the area of form and structure, there was nothing to do but wait and see what developed at the January meeting.

The first item on the January agenda concerning the question of form and structure was a motion to give second reading to the section of article 4 dealing with the criteria for establishing the twelve council districts and procedures for redistricting. After considerable debate, the commission voted to make several changes in the wording of section 4.03. One concerned the criteria that were to govern the drawing of council districts. The phrasing "population equality . . . as near as reasonably practicable" was substituted for precise limits placed upon the percentage of deviation from mathematical equality that would be tolerated. No objections were raised about requiring all districts to be "compact and contiguous." And the commission went along with the recommendation that, within the limits imposed by these criteria, all council districts ought to reflect such additional considerations as community or diversity of interests, relative rates of population growth, and patterns of social and economic interests. The only other significant change was to designate the council of the merged government as the group responsible for performing all future decennial redistrictings rather than establish an independent commission to do the job.[1]

Neither of these changes challenged the basic emphasis upon district representation. In fact, the version of section 4.03 that was given second reading specifically referred to the establishment of twelve single-member districts based on the criteria prescribed. More importantly the five new appointees consistently voted with the majority to adopt the revised, but clearly district-oriented, version of section 4.03 that had been developed during the Underwood era.

The only question remaining was whether the "new" commission would go along with the strong-mayor idea. The first signal of what was likely to happen came during a discussion of several minor wording changes that the executive committee wanted to make in section 4.07. Edgar Wallace used this occasion to get the commission to reconsider his previously rejected idea of allowing the council to select the vice-mayor from its entire membership rather than from only the three at-large members. Although the commission resoundingly defeated the Wallace motion, the critical thing was the reasoning behind the vote. Every speech against the Wallace proposal, including those made by several Pettit appointees, stressed the following point: since the commission was probably going to endorse the idea of a strong mayor, it was imperative that the person who would assume the powers of the mayor in the event of death, resignation, or absence from the community be someone who had been elected by the same community-wide constituency that had elected the mayor.

After the vote on the Wallace proposal, it did not surprise anyone that the proposed sections of article 5 establishing a strong mayor-council system were given a perfunctory and unchallenged first reading.[2] There were to be numerous conflicts over the precise wording of these sections in the months that followed. And there was still the problem of hammering out those sections of article 5 concerning the powers and duties of the chief administrative officer (CAO). But for the moment there did not seem to be any major challenge brewing over the idea of a strong mayor-council system, tempered with the "reform" notion of a highly professional CAO.

There were ten Pettit appointees on the commission at the February meeting. Following a discussion of several sections of article 2 dealing with taxing and service districts, the commission turned its attention to the second reading of article 5. Section 5.01, establishing the office of mayor as the chief executive of the merged government, was passed unanimously. In addition, the commission quickly rejected a request by a spectator to have the mayor elected on a partisan ballot, affirmed the executive committee's recommendation to pay the mayor $25,000 per year, and adopted an amendment from the floor to change the required council vote to override a veto by the mayor from two-thirds to three-fifths.[3]

Only two of the proposed sections of article 5 created any difficulty. Section 5.04 setting forth the powers of the mayor other than those pertaining to veto powers was tabled.[4] The problem was essentially procedural. The proposed section made several references to the relationship between the mayor and the chief administrative officer, and the commission simply wanted to consider these references along with the provisions of sections 5.09 and 5.10 dealing with the selection, tenure, and powers of the CAO which were still in the process of being prepared by the executive committee.

Section 5.08, on the power of the mayor to appoint administrative aides and personal secretaries, was also tabled. The proposal called for these positions to be exempted from the as yet uncompleted sections of the charter concerning the classified civil service. Even the executive committee had become less enamored with this idea after Mayor Pettit's personal secretary, Mrs. Charlene Summers, was appointed to the commission in late January and drafted by the chairman to serve on the executive committee.

As explained to the executive committee by Mrs. Summers and reiterated by Mayor Pettit at the February 15 meeting of the full commission, the proposed version of section 5.08 would effectively preclude the first mayor of the new government from considering anyone for these positions who held a civil service position under either the old or the new system of government. What civil service employee, they asked, would risk the loss of tenure and pension rights to take a job in the mayor's office?

After the February 15 meeting of the commission, the executive committee developed an amended version of section 5.08. It stipulated that "any secretary appointed by the Mayor. . . . who [was] covered by the classified civil service provisions of the Charter [would] retain all of the rights and benefits thereof."[5] All other secretaries appointed by the mayor were to be exempt from the civil service provisions. All administrative aides, *regardless of their previous status,* were to be exempt from the classified civil service. (None of Pettit's administrative assistants who might have considered retaining their position under merger were civil service employees of the city.) This was a solution the full commission could support at its March 21 meeting without disrupting the basic format of article 5.

The decision to postpone action on section 5.04 posed an entirely different set of problems for the staff and the members of the executive committee. Although the vote to table section 5.04 at the February meeting was prompted primarily by procedural considerations, it led to a complete review by the executive committee of a question that had been debated and wrestled with for months. Just how much power and independence ought to be granted to a CAO under an essentially strong mayor system?

No one really expected that the task of combining the "unreformed" idea of a strong mayor system with the basic tenets of the council-manager idea would be easy. From the very beginning of its deliberations on the subject, however, the executive committee agreed on one basic point. "Reformism" would be stressed when it came to specifying the rules governing the selection and tenure of the CAO; but when it came to defining the powers and duties of the mayor vis à vis those of the CAO, the emphasis should be placed upon preserving the basic objectives of the strong mayor system.

In keeping with the first part of this basic formula, the executive committee decided to include the following recommendations in its draft of section 5.09 to be submitted to the commission for first reading on March 21, 1972:

(a) The CAO would be hired by the council of the merged government on the recommendation of a committee composed of the mayor and four council members appointed by the vice-mayor.

(b) Candidates for the position of CAO would be required to have "demonstrable educational and/or professional experience in the art and science of governmental management."

(c) Any person hired as a CAO could be removed during the first year of service by a three-fifths vote of the council.

(d) Thereafter, the CAO could be removed for "sufficient cause or willful neglect of duty," following a public hearing, by a three-fifths vote of the council.

(e) The council could simply fire the CAO after one year by a three-fifths vote if it gave six months notice or six months severance pay.

Lexington City Manager Edgar Maroney seemed pleased with these recommendations, but he was not very happy about the idea of casting the power relationship between the mayor and the CAO in favor of the mayor.[6] His preferences were not always easy to sort out. But after several protracted sessions with the executive committee, it began to dawn on most members that Maroney wanted a series of provisions in section 5.10 granting the CAO most of the classical textbook powers of a city manager over budgets and personnel, and the supervision of all executive departments.

While the executive committee was basically disposed toward stressing the role of the mayor in each of these areas, Maroney wanted no part of such a move. His attitude began to harden, and he became condescending toward the committee in his efforts to instruct various members about the virtues of a "true" city-manager system.

In the end, Maroney's attitude and behavior probably influenced the committee's decision to recommend that the CAO be placed in a subservient position relative to the mayor all up and down the line. The final version of section 5.10 adopted for submission to the full commission in March included the following ideas:

(a) The CAO, *subject to the authority of the mayor,* would supervise the day-to-day operations of all executive departments.

(b) The CAO would *recommend to the mayor* the names of persons to be appointed as commissioners (heads) of all executive departments.

(c) The CAO would *recommend to the mayor* the content of the annual operating and capital improvements budgets.

In addition, the committee recommended that section 5.04, tabled at the February meeting of the commission, be amended to reflect the consultative nature of the powers of the CAO.

Maroney was not present at the March 21 meeting of the commission. However, several significant amendments were passed that seemed to strengthen the hand of the CAO. The mayor was required to submit to the council a written statement about the qualifications of any proposed appointee for a position as a department commissioner along with a written statement from the CAO on the same subject. Such a requirement, it was argued, would give the CAO a chance to compare the qualifications of the person nominated by the mayor with those of any other person the CAO had initially recommended to the mayor. A similar theme was struck as section 5.04 was amended to require the mayor to submit to the council an annual operating and capital improvements budget along with any budgetary recommendations by the CAO that were at variance with those submitted by the mayor. Again, the idea was to give the council a chance to evaluate the recommendations of both the political and professional leaders of the executive branch.[7]

No charter can satisfy all parties completely. City Manager Edgar Maroney was unhappy about the final version of the power relationship between the mayor and the CAO passed by the commission. Mayor Pettit was not entirely happy about the provisions regarding the selection and tenure of the CAO. And a number of commission members, including the author, wondered how the "hybrid" system would work out in practice.

With the passage of articles 4 and 5, the basic form and structure of the proposed urban county government was set. The only task remaining, as one observer joked, was to draft about a dozen more articles to flesh out what had been decided up to this point.

One of the things that had to be done was to define the boundaries of an initial set of twelve council districts according to the criteria set forth in article 4. Since the commission had decided to require a complete redistricting following each decennial census, it seemed reasonable to put the descriptions of the initial council districts in an appendix so that they would not clutter the main body of the charter forever. Besides, there was no reason to hold up the passage of article 4 until this complicated task could be done. The important thing was to get the criteria spelled out so that someone could begin to draw maps according to a fixed set of principles.

It is very difficult for anyone who has never tried to draw a set of single-member districts to understand just how complicated and politically sensitive the task can be. Everyone has a "better" way to draw district boundaries, even if required to make them contiguous, compact, and reasonably equal in population. Such additional criteria as community or diversity of interests, relative rates of growth, and patterns of social and economic interests may help to reduce the range of choices available. But they certainly do not close off debate over what constitutes an acceptable districting arrangement.

Fortunately, the Lexington commission was spared a protracted and bitter debate over this question. Several factors helped ease the pain of drawing the initial set of council districts. First, despite their obvious ambiguities, the criteria set forth in section 4.03 provided a much cleaner set of guidelines for drawing districts than most state legislatures had before them either under state law or under the myriad United States Supreme Court decisions that had been rendered on the subject of representation since *Baker* v. *Carr* up to that point.

Second, this initial set of decisions about how to apply the criteria in section 4.03 was made by a citizen commission and not an elected legislative body. This did not mean that the task was any less political in terms of its impact upon various interests in the local community. But with one or two possible exceptions, the decision-makers were not looking at the problem from the perspective of what impact the final districting plan would have upon their own electoral fortunes in the future.[8] (It will be interesting to observe how the redistricting process based on these same criteria will be handled by the Urban County Council following the 1980 census.)

Finally, the Lexington commission acquired the services of Dr.

Malcolm Jewell, one of the nation's leading scholars in the field of legislative representation, to supervise the preparation of Appendix A. Shortly after he was appointed to the commission by Mayor Pettit in January 1972, the chairman asked him to serve on the executive committee and to head a subcommittee charged with preparing a set of council district maps based on the criteria set forth in section 4.03.

Jewell accepted the challenge and attacked the problem with zeal and dedication. On March 14, three weeks after the full commission had given second reading to section 4.03, he presented a set of maps to the executive committee.

Jewell had often been called upon by legislative bodies and the federal courts for his expert advice on such matters. But I suspect he had never experienced having his recommendations received with so few reservations. Only two very minor objections were raised by the executive committee on March 14, neither of them related to the criteria in section 4.03. One was that his maps would require a complete overhaul of existing precinct boundaries. The other complaint was that his recommended council district lines did not always square with the boundary lines for state legislative districts.

Jewell pointed out that precinct lines would have to be redrawn anyway. If merger passed, it would be imperative to get rid of the precinct system that had to be tied to that crazy city boundary in order to run city and county elections. Even if this were not necessary, there would have to be major precinct changes to accommodate the alterations made in state House and Senate districts during the 1970 session of the General Assembly. Jewell agreed that it might be possible to make some adjustments that would bring his suggested council district boundaries into better conformity with the new House and Senate lines. But to eliminate all conflicts between these various sets of representational district lines would require major departures from the criteria established for the proposed urban county council districts.

With that, the executive committee agreed to endorse the Jewell report and submit it for first reading at the March 21 meeting of the full commission. The only stipulation attached was that Jewell and the executive committee would attempt to work out the needed changes to bring the recommended district boundaries more in line with the new House and Senate districts before second reading.

The full commission gave first reading to Jewell's proposal including the aforementioned stipulation on March 21. And it passed a slightly revised version of his maps based on that stipulation following the debate on second reading at its meeting on April 18. The vote was twenty-six to zero, with one member abstaining.[9]

The twelve districts would range in population from 14,116 to 14,867 people, according to 1970 United States Census figures. The average population stood at 14,527. There would be three inner-city districts, two of them predominantly black and a third about 40 percent black (Districts 1, 2, and 3 respectively in Figure 2). District 5 contained an older "suburban" section of the community, while Districts 6, 7, 10, and 11 contained mixtures of former city and county suburban areas that had been developed more recently. Districts 8 and 9 represented the newest and most rapidly growing built-up areas in the community. District 12 was predominantly rural in character.

District 4 was the least homogeneous. It contained a large contingent of University of Kentucky students, several older blue-collar neighborhoods, a couple of older upper-income areas, and a number of transitional areas.[10] In terms of its active electorate, however, it was reasonably homogeneous since most of the university students who were included by the United States Census as residents of the area were not registered voters in Fayette County.[11]

The adoption of Appendix A on April 18, 1972, marked the completion of all major aspects of the charter dealing with the representative branch of the proposed government. But the commission and its executive committee had also been working on a variety of matters directly related to the provisions of article 5 dealing with the mayor and the CAO.

For example, except for one section, all of the article concerning the powers and duties of those county officers to be retained after merger was given first reading in February and passed, with some minor technical revisions, the following month. No major conflicts

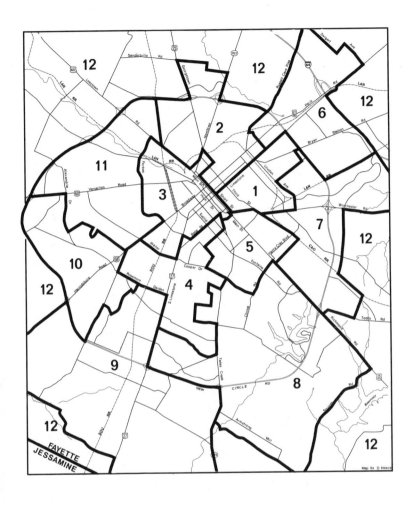

Figure 2. Council Districts under the
Lexington-Fayette Urban County Government

arose over those parts of article 11 dealing with such constitutional officers as county attorney, sheriff, jailer, court clerk, or property valuation officer. All simply retained their former powers and duties. The sheriff was made the chief tax collector for the proposed urban county government. The county jailer was made the chief detention officer for the combined city-county jail facilities. And the property valuation officer would do all assessments in the county.[12]

At the March meeting the section dealing with the powers and duties of the county judge was adopted. In order to understand the significance of this section, it is necessary to recall that under the existing system the county judge was the chief executive officer of the county government. But most of the executive and administrative authority vested in the office was based on state statutes; the constitution described the office as an essentially judicial one.[13] Under the constitution the commission had to retain the office, but it could not vest the executive powers of a new urban county government in the office of a mayor and still allow the county judge to exercise the executive and administrative authority assigned to him under state law. Having decided to create a strong, elected chief executive known as the mayor, the commission reduced the county judge to essentially a judicial officer within the unified court system that it eventually provided for in article 10.[14] This seemed to satisfy the state constitutional requirements regarding the office, while at the same time avoiding any conflict over who would be the chief executive officer of the new government.

On the surface it might appear that the commission was quite divided on the future role of the existing legislative body in the county government known as the Fiscal Court. It refused to give first reading to the section covering this matter at the February meeting and final action was not completed until April. However, most of the debate concerned how far the commission could safely go toward stripping the Fiscal Court of its statutory legislative and executive authority, and how much salary ought to be specified in the charter for the three county commissioners who, along with the county judge, made up the Fayette County Fiscal Court. In the end, the full commission pushed the executive committee to trim further the powers of this body under merger and to specify that the three county commissioners would receive no compensation for their newly defined and quite limited duties.[15]

Some members of the commission did worry privately about the impact of these decisions upon the position the incumbents of these offices might take during a referendum on the proposed charter. To judge by the experience of other communities, these elected officials might fight merger tooth and nail to prevent a major reduction of their power. At minimum, stripping the county judge and the Fiscal Court of virtually all of their legislative and executive powers would not seem to be the best way to go about winning their support for the charter.

Yet Judge Robert Stephens not only acquiesced to these decisions, but he became one of the most vigorous supporters of the charter during the ensuing referendum campaign. As for the three county commissioners, they studied the draft of section 11.02 prior to the April 18 meeting of the charter commission and reportedly found it quite acceptable.[16]

As an observer of merger efforts in other communities and a participant in the drafting of the Lexington charter, I found it difficult to understand this seemingly unusual behavior on the part of Judge Stephens and the members of the Fayette County Fiscal Court. Political scientists are notorious cynics about the motives of politicians. But at the time, there was no hard evidence to support even the least cynical hypotheses one could conjure up. Even the speculation that perhaps these particular politicians had nothing to lose by supporting a cause that had only about one chance in four of ever becoming a reality (on the basis of the record in other settings to date) did not seem satisfactory. Why would anyone in their position want to risk even a remote chance that the charter would pass in order to placate a few "do-gooders" in the community?

The only argument that seemed to make any sense was that these people were sincere in their assertions that they wanted the right thing for the community. In the light of subsequent events, this may still provide at least a partial answer to the puzzle. But it should also be noted that shortly after the proposed charter had been adopted by the voters, one member of the Fayette County Fiscal

Court confirmed the rumor that he would retire from local political office at the end of his term in December of 1973. (The charter, if passed, would go into effect on January 1, 1974.) Another subsequently announced that he would run for an at-large seat on the new council, and the third said he would seek to represent District 12 on the new council.[17]

Judge Stephens considered running for mayor under the new charter, but did not press the matter after it became clear that Mayor Pettit was also after the job. Instead he ran for another term as county judge, despite the limitations imposed upon his former powers by the new charter. Some local political sages maintained that he wanted to ensure himself another election victory rather than risk any future ambitions for higher political office in what probably would have been a very close race with Pettit. (Stephens eventually sought and won a statewide office in 1975 as attorney general of Kentucky.) Whatever the reasons, the merger commission had overcome one of the major remaining obstacles to making the strong-mayor idea workable without invoking the wrath of the county judge or the members of the Fiscal Court. The only major hurdle left was the devising of an institutional framework for organizing the executive branch under a strong-mayor system.

This final step in the process of fleshing out the strong-mayor idea involved drafting two related articles. One article would spell out the organization of the major executive departments and divisions that would operate under the supervision of the mayor and the CAO. The other would fit various independent boards, commissions, and authorities into the total executive structure.

It is hard to say exactly when the executive committee started to work on articles 6 and 7. Many ideas directly relevant to the contents of these articles had been raised before March 7, 1972, when the committee formally began its deliberations on organizing the executive branch. Much of the informal discussion prior to March 7 came during the preparation of those parts of article 5 that referred to the power of the mayor and CAO to supervise all executive departments and agencies. But other scattered discussions of the subject dated back to the summer of 1971.

In fact, it was the scattered and informal nature of these discussions that made it so difficult for the executive committee to begin its formal deliberations on articles 6 and 7 with any degree of consensus about where it was heading. There were many logical ways to organize the functions of local government into departments, divisions, or agencies; and everyone seemed to have a more logical way to do the job.

Fortunately the committee recognized the problem and decided to start at the top and try to define a set of broad functional areas that might serve as a basis for organizing executive departments. Eric Karnes suggested that, on the basis of the previous discussions of the committee, there ought to be six functional categories established as a starting point. His motion called for starting with finance, public safety, parks and recreation, human services, public works, and legal affairs. Mayor Pettit, who was at the March 7 meeting, urged the committee to add a seventh category—housing and community development.

After considerable discussion concerning the kinds of specific activities of local government that would fit logically under each of these broad headings, the committee adopted an amended version of the Karnes motion to include Pettit's idea. The chairman and the staff were then asked to prepare a detailed proposal based on this motion. In addition, the committee asked the staff to draw up a proposal about how various independent boards, commissions, and authorities might fit into the basic scheme it had outlined. Although no vote was taken on the matter, there did seem to be rather widespread support for the idea cf reducing the number of independent boards and placing many of their activities under line departments.

For the next three weeks the staff worked almost night and day on the problem. A 34-page proposal entitled "A Plan for the Executive Branch of the Lexington-Fayette Urban County Government" was prepared and distributed to the members of the committee at its meeting on March 28. Its contents, however, had been discussed with each member of the committee, either in person or by telephone, prior to its distribution. The general consensus seemed to be that the staff was on the right track and that the committee would probably stand behind most of the proposals, including the recommendation to have an office of administrative services under the direct supervision of the cao.[18]

Several substantive changes were made by the executive committee at its meeting on March 28, most of them aimed at keeping children's services separate from juvenile probation and detention activities.[19] Questions were raised about a number of other parts of the "Plan," but they did not result in motions to change what had been recommended by the staff. In addition, the commission adopted a motion by the chairman to schedule a special meeting of the full commission to hear the views of those who would be most directly affected by the "Plan" before moving ahead with the actual drafting of articles 6 and 7.

By the end of that week the staff had either hand-delivered or mailed copies of the "Plan" to every local agency, board, and commission along with an invitation to appear at a public hearing on its contents scheduled for the evening of April 12, 1972. Although it had been disappointed in previous attempts to solicit the views of agency heads and board chairmen, the commission hoped that there would be a more positive response to this invitation.

But despite elaborate preparations that included moving the meeting to a larger auditorium, only a small group appeared on April 12. Actually, there were more merger commission members on the stage than people in the audience. And the representatives of local agencies who came prepared to discuss the "Plan" tended to be those who had given the most input while it was being prepared. Most other agency representatives who came wanted to talk about what was going to happen to their pensions.

It was a very disappointing evening for the twenty-eight members of the commission who attended the special meeting. For some, including many members of the executive committee, disappointment turned into anger. The apparent lack of interest on the part of so many people who were in a position to say whether the "Plan" was workable was a bitter pill to swallow. Perhaps this helps to explain why the executive committee decided to submit, without review, the staff-prepared drafts of articles 6 and 7 based on the "Plan" to the full commission for first reading on April 18.

It may even help to explain why the twenty-seven members present at the April 18 meeting voted unanimously to give both of these proposed articles first reading in almost record time.[20]

Tempers cooled a bit after that, and the executive committee set to work on polishing several rough spots in the drafts of articles 6 and 7. But the committee made no major alterations nor did the full commission take exception to the basic contents of the proposals. It did labor long and hard on some relatively minor technical changes, but it managed to complete action on most parts of articles 6 and 7 at its meeting in May.

Two substantive questions did pose several problems for the commission: the proposal to abolish the local public housing authority and vest its responsibilities in a separate division under the Department of Housing and Community Development, and a proposal to do the same thing with the local urban renewal agency. Both matters were tabled at the May meeting.

In both cases, the commission seemed prepared to go along with the proposed method for handling public housing and urban renewal. The commission had, after all, taken a hard line against retaining any independent board, commission, or authority (other than purely advisory ones) unless a good case could be made that it would be *legally* indefensible to transfer their functions to a regular line department. Thus, it opted to abolish the executive board which ran the former county children's services agency and the County Board of Parks and Recreation.[21] In both cases their executive and administrative powers were to be vested in a line department. Along the same lines, it had voted to move the entire professional staff of the Lexington-Fayette County Planning Commission into the new Division of Planning in the Department of Housing and Community Development. The planning commission would retain all of its powers, but it would have to rely on the Division of Planning for technical and professional services.

On the other hand the commission had voted to retain an independent transit authority, library board, and airport board. There was no way under Kentucky law to maintain public transit systems, libraries, or airports except under the direct control of an independent board or authority.

The real question in the case of public housing and urban renewal was whether they, too, legally had to be administered by independent agencies. In the case of public housing, lawyers representing the federal government sent the commission letters suggesting that there would be serious legal problems if this essentially federally funded activity in the local community was tampered with. Reluctantly, in June the commission conceded and passed a revised version of the appropriate sections in articles 6 and 7.

Urban renewal proved to be a bit more complicated. Mrs. Jenny Bryant, who headed the local urban renewal agency, had met with the executive committee on the matter, but offered no strong legal arguments against the proposal to abolish her agency and move it into a regular line department. She told the committee that it might lead to difficulties if her agency's bonding obligations had to be transferred. But she conceded that state law seemed to give local governments the option of conducting urban renewal either under an independent agency or under a line department. She repeated her arguments at the June meeting of the full commission, stressing once again that it might be technically and operationally more convenient to leave things as they were because of the bonding problem. But the commission was more impressed with the provisions of the state statute and voted to pass the proposal recommended by the executive committee.[22]

Space will not permit a full description of passage of the final details of articles 6 and 7. But Figure 3, coupled with what has been said about the thrust of decisions regarding independent boards and commissions, provides a summary of what was done.

Many loose ends had to be tied together at the final meeting of the Lexington-Fayette County Merger Commission on June 20, 1972. The sections of articles 6 and 7 dealing with public housing and urban renewal had to be completed. Several minor wording changes had to be made in at least two other articles. And the commission had to give second reading to six other complete articles needed to round out the charter.

None of these items had evoked any major controversy and all of them seemed destined to pass by very large margins. In fact, the

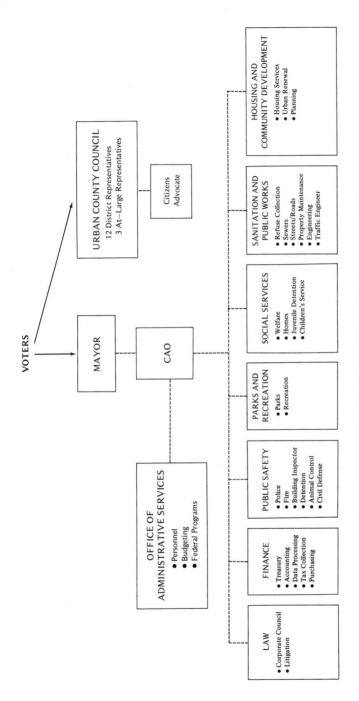

Figure 3. Basic Legislative and Executive Structure of the Lexington-Fayette Urban County Government

commission had worked through its entire agenda before any trouble erupted. After the unanimous vote to give second reading to the final article in the proposed charter, the chairman tried to insert into the record that there had been only one communication to the staff or the commission from outside persons or groups protesting any feature of the charter as it now stood. The communication in question was a letter, dated May 24, 1972, from Dr. John Trevey on behalf of the Fayette County Republican Party supporting the idea of partisan elections.

It was duly noted that the executive committee had considered Trevey's letter and had rejected his suggestion on the grounds that the subject of partisan versus nonpartisan elections had been debated and voted upon on numerous occasions. Trevey was not present at the meeting that night, but Carl Penske, a Republican who had argued the virtues of partisan elections before the commission in the past, submitted a petition urging the commission to reconsider its position on the subject. Since Penske had spent six months gathering only 124 signatures on the petition, no one on the commission believed that there was a ground swell of public sentiment in favor of partisan elections. However the commission entertained a motion to reconsider the matter in order to put the feelings of the group on record one more time. The vote to defeat the motion was unanimous. Even the two stalwart supporters of partisan elections voted against reopening a subject that had been thoroughly and openly debated on numerous occasions during the preceding fifteen months.

Several other articles were given second reading at the June meeting. Article 8 on the budgetary process was adopted without difficulty, even though it called for introducing Lexington to such things as "program budgeting" and five-year capital improvement programming. In addition, the commission adopted State Senator Joe Graves's suggestion for an independent and reasonably powerful citizen ombudsman within the new system. And so article 4 was amended to include a section creating the office of citizens' advocate, the head of which would be hired by the council to receive citizen complaints about the operation of various agencies and departments of the new government and to recommend changes based on those complaints. While the commission backed away from giving the office full subpoena powers, it did lock the position of citizens' advocate into the same selection and tenure provisions specified for the CAO. Furthermore, it wrote into the charter (in article 16) a very firm and detailed code of ethics based on the Jacksonville, Florida, charter, which would require elected and nonelected officials of the new government to be held responsible for their actions.

Finally the commission adopted a set of civil service provisions that ought to have warmed the heart of the most avid civic reformer. All former civil service employees of the former city government would retain their civil service positions, along with all rights and benefits to which they were entitled under the old system. County employees were to be brought into the classified civil service system at levels commensurate with those of employees of the former city who performed equivalent types of duties.[23] The commission also included a provision that no former county employee would receive a lower salary or wage than he had been receiving on the effective date of the charter.

Some city employees had complained that allowing former county employees to enter the civil service without subjecting them to any examination or certification requirements would lower the quality of the public service.[24] But for the most part, the concerns expressed to the commission while article 9 was being drafted centered on the question of pensions. It was exceedingly difficult to get some city employees to separate the notion of civil service from the concept of pensions. To many of these people, civil service *meant* pension benefits, and it was hard to comprehend the charter provisions aimed at allowing former county employees to enter the classified civil service, but not necessarily the pension systems that had been developed for former city employees.[25]

They grasped the point about preserving the pension rights of all former city employees, but they put little trust in the provision that no former county employee who was brought into the civil service system would automatically be entitled to become a member of any existing pension plan. Membership could be extended under the charter, but only to those former county employees who could meet the qualifications (of age, health, and the like) that any new city employee would have had to meet under the old system. Even the statement that no one would be allowed to join the existing pension plans if it might result in the "impairment, curtailment or diminishment of any right or benefit accrued" by any member of the city pension plans did not seem to allay their concerns.

The members of the commission, however, seemed anxious to ensure that employees of the new government would be under a strong civil service system, while at the same time preserving the financial integrity of existing pension systems. Furthermore, they seemed prepared to "bite the bullet" on this question even if it upset some city employees. Besides, three of Pettit's appointees to the commission were city civil service employees and active in their respective employee associations. And all three supported the proposed article 9 on personnel and pension systems.[26]

Up to this point the discussion concerning the drafting of the Lexington charter has dealt almost exclusively with how and why the local commission adopted a structural format that featured non-partisan elections, an emphasis upon district representation, and a rather novel version of the strong mayor-council system of government. However, throughout its deliberations on the questions of form and structure, the commission was also working on the complex problem of establishing an equitable system for handling existing and future variations in both tax and service packages under merger. In the next chapter, we shall examine the way in which the Lexington commission responded to the various questions posed by this problem.

7

∞∞∞∞∞∞∞∞∞∞∞∞∞∞∞∞∞∞∞∞∞∞∞∞∞∞∞∞∞∞

Taxes and Services

AT FIRST glance the tax-service situation in Lexington did not appear terribly complicated. Property owners throughout Fayette County paid a county ad valorem tax of 16.65 cents per $100 property valuation. City property owners paid an additional 61.7 cents per $100 in city ad valorem taxes.[1] On the service side of the ledger, city residents were served by the city police and fire departments while those living outside the city were served by the much smaller county police and fire departments. City residents had street lights while county residents did not. City residents had their trash and garbage picked up by the city government; county residents had to pay approximately seventy-six dollars a year to a private collector for such services. And city residents had city sanitary sewers, whereas most of those living outside the city were on private septic tanks. (Some county residents were on one of several small private sanitary sewer systems, and a few others were hooked up to the city system on a yearly fee basis.)

Had this been all there was to the tax-service situation, the task confronting the Lexington-Fayette County Merger Commission would have been relatively simple. It could have done what every other merger commission had done—namely, designate the entire county as a "general service area" with its own ad valorem tax rate and the city as an "urban service area" with an additional ad valorem tax rate to cover the costs of the additional services rendered to city residents. Beyond this it would have been necessary to prescribe a procedure for expanding the area covered by the "urban service area" in the future. Any one of a dozen or more city-county consolidation charters could have been used as a guide.

Unfortunately, the situation was not this simple. The local tax situation was much more muddled when taxes other than ad valorem taxes were taken into consideration. The Fayette County government derived approximately 76 percent of its yearly revenues from property taxes, the city only 34 percent.[2] Fifty-seven percent of the city's yearly revenues came from a 2 percent occupational license fee or "wage tax" imposed on all persons employed in the city and the equivalent fee on net profits paid by all businesses in the city.[3]

State law required that the occupational and net profits "taxes" be applied uniformly throughout the territorial jurisdiction of the proposed urban county government. This meant that it would be impossible to relate any variation in these license fees to variations in services provided under any system of service areas.

Once this was clearly understood, it became equally clear that the imposition of a county-wide wage and net profits "tax" could have major political repercussions when it came to securing the support of certain groups of voters for a merger plan or charter. While most of the labor force in Fayette County was already paying the wage "tax" by virtue of being employed in the city, a sizable number of people worked outside the city. And a large number of businesses, including all of the large and famous horse farms of the Bluegrass, were not subject to the 2 percent city net profit "tax." It would not be easy to demonstrate that the imposition of these additional "taxes" under merger would bring these businesses or their employees any immediate additions or improvements in the local government service package they were already receiving.

It was equally disconcerting to discover that a number of areas in the existing city of Lexington were not receiving all of the additional services that supposedly went with being in the city. Several older low-income and predominantly black central-city neighborhoods had never had sanitary sewers. Several recently annexed areas were still without city sewers, street lights, or both. Yet the property owners in all of these areas were paying full city property tax in addition to the county property tax. And those who rented homes in these areas undoubtedly had the additional tax passed on to them in their rent.

Then there were the service problems posed by that zigzagging city boundary. As it meandered across the face of metropolitan Lexington, it excluded numerous enclaves of built-up areas from such services as street lights and sanitary sewers. Some of these areas had been developed many decades before, and many of them needed or wanted one or more of the urban services available to most city residents. Furthermore, some county residents were in fact receiving some city services, but for reasons no one seemed able to explain, had never been annexed or put on the city tax rolls.

Finally it ought to be recalled that greater Lexington was a very rapidly growing area and was experiencing all the problems associated with rapid urban growth, including urban sprawl, scattered site development, and several noteworthy "fish and chips" strip developments. For some, the by-products of growth compounded the problem of defining an urban service area that would square with the boundaries of existing taxing jurisdictions.

For others, the growth of the community also meant wrestling with the problem of how merger might better serve the goal of achieving orderly growth. Could the tax-service provisions of the merger charter be written in such a way as to curtail the development of new subdivisions and commercial sites far removed from existing sewer lines, street lights, and mass transit routes? Could a flexible tax-service system be designed to allow for the expansion of additional urban services on a selective basis according to the needs and desires of those living in existing and proposed high-density areas of the county?

Most of these problems and concerns were basically understood by the time the executive committee took up the question of taxes and services in September 1971. Others became evident as the details of the Lexington situation were raised for discussion. As might be expected, the initial debates on these problems tended to be quite disorganized. Eventually, however, the problems began to fall into some sort of order, and the executive committee began to attack them in a more systematic fashion.

The first and perhaps most crucial decision was to acknowledge the impossibility of equalizing the service package offered to all residents of Fayette County under merger within the near future. Rural areas did not need or want street lights or sanitary sewers, and they certainly did not need to bear the extra expense of providing such things as hook-and-ladder fire trucks. Some of the built-up areas outside the city were, for the moment, getting along on septic tanks. And some of them neither needed nor wanted such urban services as street lights. Furthermore, it would take time, money, and much legal flexibility for a new merged government to extend such services even to those areas that did need or want them.

Once this was established, the committee took up the task of defining an initial set of service districts that would reflect the best possible delineation of the existing variations between city and county services. After a careful review of the situation, including the service inequities that existed in some city neighborhoods, it was decided that the least amount of variation in local government service packages could be obtained if service districts were defined, at least initially, in terms of the existing boundary between the city and the county.

Thus, the committee decided to recommend the creation of a General Services District (GSD) that would embrace all residents of the area to be served by the proposed merged government. In addition, it recommended the creation of a Full Urban Services District (FUSD) that would initially embrace only those residents living within the existing city boundary. In short, on the day merger took effect, the residents of the former city of Lexington would be in both the GSD and the FUSD. Those living outside the former city would be in only the GSD.

The basic idea was that the GSD would provide all residents of the community with such general governmental services as parks, libraries, courts, mass transit, airports, streets and roads, welfare and social services, refuse and garbage disposal, basic police and fire protection services, and basic code enforcement programs. Those living in the FUSD would receive such additional services as street lights, street cleaning, refuse and garbage collection, sanitary sewers, and such additional police and fire protection services as might be required. (According to the debates of the committee, the last item meant whatever additional police and fire personnel and equipment that might be needed to serve very high density areas.)

In a related set of decisions, the committee also recommended that the commission relate these basic variations in service packages to the existing variations in the ad valorem tax rates imposed upon residents of city and county. Seizing the opportunity afforded by the recently adopted section 172A of the state constitution, the committee recommended that the initial ad valorem tax rate within the GSD be set at the same level imposed by the Fayette County Fiscal Court at the time the proposed charter went into effect and that there be an additional ad valorem tax rate imposed within the FUSD equal to that imposed by the city of Lexington on the effective date of the charter.

Neither of these decisions by the executive committee proved to be controversial. Neither of them marked any radical departure from what other merger charter commissions had done or, for that matter, from the status quo.

But when the committee took up the question of how and under what conditions the proposed merged government might extend urban services into new areas in the future, it began to confront difficulties. The first major stumbling block appeared when the committee tried to borrow some ideas from several other charters concerning the expansion of the FUSD. All charters consulted allowed the council of the consolidated government to designate areas to be included in the urban services district and impose the additional property tax rate for that district within a specified period of time (usually one year) before all of the additional urban services were installed.

Several committee members took exception to the idea of imposing additional taxes before any additional services were rendered. After considerable haggling, they convinced the full committee to recommend that no additional property tax rate be levied in any area designated for inclusion in the FUSD until all of the additional services specified for that district were installed and operative.

While this move eliminated any time lag in applying the principle of taxes related to services received, it did promise to compound one of the major problems confronting several other existing consolidated governments that had been studied by the staff of the

Lexington commission. Expanding the FUSD meant that a consolidated government had to install *all* of the additional services specified for that district. Although most of these charters allowed the consolidated government to collect the higher property tax rate for a period of one year prior to installation of the additional services, even twelve months is a very short period of time within which to complete all of the financial, engineering, and administrative details involved in installing an entire package of urban services.

The experience of Nashville seemed to be particularly salient on this point. The mere necessity of installing *all* additional services to any area designated for inclusion in the urban service area seemed to have had a debilitating effect on the expansion of urban services in the greater Nashville area ever since its charter went into effect in 1963. This was not only the conclusion of the Lexington commission's staff in the fall of 1971, but it was to be very forcefully reiterated by Nashville Mayor Beverly Briley before a merger campaign rally held in Lexington on October 11, 1972.[4]

The implications of this problem seemed to point toward the need for a more flexible way to extend urban services to new areas than could be achieved by simply designating some procedure for expanding the FUSD. This need became especially clear when the executive committee began to consider the selected needs and desires of various neighborhoods in the area outside that haphazard city boundary that was to serve as the initial boundary for the FUSD.

After much discussion, the executive committee recommended that the proposed urban county council have the option of creating a series of Partial Urban Services Districts (PUSD) for the purpose of providing one or more of the additional urban services specified for the FUSD. This would allow the council to extend urban services on a selective and piecemeal basis to areas that needed or wanted them without having to install all of the additional services of the FUSD. Thus, the council could create a "partial" district in one area to provide street lights, in another to provide sanitary sewers. It could also provide any combination of urban services that would fall short of the total package offered in the FUSD. In each case, the committee recommended that the council be allowed to impose an additional property tax in a "partial" district only after such services were installed, and at a rate that would be commensurate with the kind, type and level of additional services provided.

Despite the innovative character of the PUSD concept, the committee seemed reasonably well satisfied with its work up to this point. It had confronted the basic variations in the existing property tax and governmental services by recommending the creation of a General Services District and an initial Full Urban Services District, each with its own property tax burden. And it had provided a highly flexible way to expand urban services into new areas either through the expansion of the FUSD or the creation of Partial Urban Services Districts. The latter seemed a particularly neat way to handle the problems posed by the irregular city boundary.

There were, however, several very serious problems that none of these recommendations could solve. None of them, for example, did anything about the problem of extending the concept of relating taxes to services to those areas within the existing city that were not receiving all services specified for the initial FUSD. Since these areas were already subjected to the additional property tax rate levied by the city, the recommended provisions regarding the property tax burden to be imposed upon the FUSD would simply have perpetuated the existing tax-service inequities within these former city areas after the merger charter was put into effect.

The pressure was on the executive committee to propose restricting the expansion of the FUSD or the creation of any PUSD until all areas within the existing city limits were receiving all of the services designated for the initial FUSD. Some members of the committee were reluctant to endorse such a recommendation, but the generalized support for the concept of relating taxes to services, coupled with an inability on the part of the staff or the members of the executive committee to come up with a viable alternative, led to the adoption of this concept.

Soon several members of the executive committee began thinking about how the principle of restricting the expansion of the FUSD or the creation of "partial districts" might also be used to promote a more orderly approach to urban growth. The major device for containing urban growth available to local decision-makers at the time was the concept of the "Urban Service Area" that had been developed by the local city-county planning commission. As shown in Figure 4 the planning commission had designated a rather large, but exceedingly compact, portion of Fayette County as the area within which all urban development ought to be confined within the foreseeable future. But the concept of an "Urban Service Area" did not have the force of law, and the integrity of the concept had been violated on several occasions.

At the urging of several members of the Lexington-Fayette County Planning Commission staff and several members of the executive committee, it was agreed that the proposed article 2 ought to include a provision restricting the council from expanding the FUSD or creating any PUSD outside the Urban Service Area. The idea was to use the proposed merger charter to transform the concept of an Urban Service Area into a legally enforceable guide to future growth and development. It was hoped that this would put an end to the pressure on local elected officials to grant favorable zoning decisions to certain developers who insisted upon placing high-density projects on scattered sites far removed from existing urban services.

No one on the executive committee believed it would be easy to "sell" the entire package of recommendations contained in its proposed article 2 to the full commission. It contained too many complex ideas and raised too many sensitive issues to warrant optimism about its becoming part of the proposed charter without major revision. Nevertheless, the committee did get the full commission to give the proposed article, including the controversial sections, first reading at its November 1971 meeting.

With only a bare quorum of sixteen members in attendance at the December 1971 meeting of the full commission, only the least contentious sections of the proposed article 2 gained the required consent of all members present. Thus it was quickly agreed that the sections dealing with the idea of having two initial services districts (a GSD and a FUSD), each with its own ad valorem tax rate, ought to be given second reading. In effect, the commission had agreed to

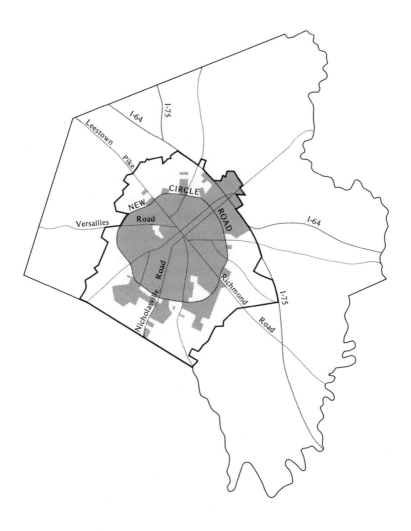

Figure 4. Urban Service Area. Shading shows areas of heaviest residential, commercial, and industrial development as of 1970.

an initial set of taxing and services districts that would closely approximate the status quo.

In the process of passing these sections, the commission also endorsed a very general reference to the possibility of having Partial Urban Services Districts. While quite innovative in its implications, the reference to PUSD that was passed merely empowered the council of the merged government to create such districts. It said nothing about the conditions governing the creation of such districts or the tax rates to be applied should the council exercise its power to create such entities.

In fact, the proposed restrictions upon the expansion of the FUSD and the creation of "partial districts" brought the commission to a halt. The idea of forbidding the expansion of additional urban services until all residents of the city were receiving all of the services that went with being in the FUSD was denounced as impractical and overstringent. So was the proposal to limit the expansion of the FUSD and the creation of "partial districts" to the area designated by the planning commission as the Urban Service Area.

As the debate proceeded, however, it became clear that there was a rather strong core of support for the basic objectives that these proposed restrictions were ostensibly designed to achieve. But it was equally clear that with only sixteen members present it was going to be impossible to give second reading to any proposal even remotely affected by these two ideas. As the chances of unanimity faded, members of the executive committee introduced a series of motions to table all remaining sections of the proposed article 2. (A motion to table was a procedural matter and could be passed by a simple majority of those present and voting; there may not have been enough votes to give second reading to these sections, but there were more than enough votes to keep them alive for future consideration as the motions to table passed by votes of fifteen to one and sixteen to zero.)[5]

It is useless to speculate about whether a large turnout at this meeting would have resulted in the passage of more sections of article 2. With only sixteen members present, the commission was unable to do more than endorse the general outline of an initial system of taxing and services districts that closely approximated the status quo. All other portions of the proposed article had to be added to the list of issues that had been considered but left unresolved during the Underwood era.

Twenty-three members, including five new appointees, attended the regular monthly meeting on January 18, 1972. A motion to remove the relevant sections of article 2 from the table was passed without dissent. A motion to give second reading to these sections was made and seconded. Edgar Wallace then attempted to resurrect the restriction, voted down in December, on expanding the FUSD until all areas of the city had received all of the additional services they were entitled to. But his motion was quickly defeated by a vote of twenty-one to one with one abstention. With that, the commission gave second reading to all of the sections that had been tabled in December, without the proposed restrictions.[6]

In addition to making major progress toward completing article 2, the commission supplied the members of the executive committee with several vital bits of information. For one thing, the wide-ranging debate on the subject of taxing and services districts that night clearly indicated that the level of support for restricting the expansion of urban services to the Urban Service Area had fallen almost to zero. For some the proposed restriction was simply too stringent. For others it implied granting the local planning commission unprecedented legal power to decide when and where future growth and development would take place. For still others it implied further complication of the already complicated concept of "full" and "partial" urban services districts within a General Services District. Finally, there were those who felt that, regardless of the merits associated with the objective that was being sought, the problem of orderly growth was the kind of policy question that ought to be left to elected officials and not be "solved" by the provisions of a basic charter for organizing a system of government.

On a more positive note, the debate on article 2 revealed that there was still considerable interest in finding a fair solution to the problem confronting those who were included in the initial FUSD but were not receiving all of the additional services specified for that district. While the Wallace solution to the problem had been resoundingly defeated, this was not because most of the commission members wanted to ignore the problem.

Two major objections cost Wallace a victory. First, any attempt to restrict the expansion of urban services to areas outside the former city until all city residents were receiving the total urban service package would force the new merged government to install certain services on a crash basis without providing the resources to do the job. This would be a particularly difficult problem, according to some spokesmen, when it became necessary to install sanitary sewers in very low-income areas under conventional financing practices. (At the time the question was raised, the availability of federal funds to install sewer lines in low-income areas was very doubtful.)

The second objection was a legal one. As the debate proceeded, several members of the commission expressed concern that the Wallace idea might strengthen the possibility that those residents who were not receiving all of the services they were entitled to could sue the new merged government. The city of Lexington had never made a legal commitment to provide every city resident with such services as sanitary sewers or street lights, but the proposed charter would definitely commit the consolidated government to provide these and other specified urban services within the FUSD, which was initially to embrace all of the territory of the former city of Lexington. The Wallace proposal would reinforce that legal claim by stipulating that none of these additional urban services could be extended to former county residents until the merged government had complied with the provisions concerning the kinds of services that were to be supplied to every resident of the initial FUSD.

Several alternatives to the Wallace solution to the problem were explored by the executive committee at its meeting on January 25, 1972. One was simply to redefine the boundary of the initial FUSD to exclude those areas of the city that were not currently receiving all of the services specified for the FUSD. The basic difficulty with this approach was that the areas in question were in various sections of the city. In addition, there was considerable variation in the actual urban services available in these areas. All of them received such services as garbage collection, street cleaning, and city police and fire protection. However, some of them also had street lights but not city sewers, while others were on the city sewer system, but did not have street lights.

Therefore, these areas could not simply be excluded from the initial FUSD and placed in the GSD only. In terms of services, they were somewhere between the service packages prescribed for these two basic districts. Consequently, it would have been necessary to designate each of these widely scattered areas as an initial PUSD. To do this, the commission would have to write into the proposed charter a detailed description of each PUSD; the kind, type, and level of additional services that were being provided in each of these "partial districts"; and a detailed statement of the ad valorem tax rate to be applied in each case.

The more this alternative was discussed, the more obvious it became that the commission had neither the time nor the staff resources to pursue the matter. Moreover, the entire project flew in the face of what Rufus Lisle and others regarded as a fundamental principle—that a merger charter should provide a basic outline of how a consolidated government ought to be organized and oriented. This particular proposal, it was argued, exceeded any reasonable interpretation of that principle.

One variable in the total equation could be manipulated without precluding the expansion of needed urban services to county residents, while at the same time avoiding the necessity of including detailed descriptions of an initial set of "partial districts" in the proposed charter. That variable was the property tax rate. The commission staff and several members of the executive committee at a meeting on January 25, 1972, hit upon the idea of simply inserting a statement lowering the property tax rate on all properties in the initial FUSD as defined originally that were not receiving all of the additional services prescribed for that district. One suggestion was to allow these property owners to petition the merged government for a reduction in their ad valorem tax rate commensurate with the kind, type, and levels of additional services they were receiving. Another suggestion was to make the tax cut automatic by requiring the council of the merged government to lower the rate within a specified period of time, making the rate commensurate with the kind, type, and levels of services provided.

At this point, the executive committee charged the chairman with the task of developing a detailed proposal based on the principle of reducing the property tax. The chairman in turn co-opted the services of William McCann, one of the first five Pettit appointees to the commission and one of those selected by the chairman to fill a vacancy on the executive committee in January of 1972. He was also the coauthor of KRS 67A (the Peak-McCann bill) under which the commission operated and the person who had raised the question concerning the right of certain former city residents to sue the merged government for not rendering all the services specified in the proposed charter for those living in the initial FUSD.

During the next two weeks, these two met frequently. The results of their efforts marked a major turning point in the long and contentious controversy over the final contents of article 2. They urged the executive committee to propose the following amendment to section 2.02 of the proposed article on taxing and services districts: "In the event that any area or property located within the initial Full Urban Services District is not provided with one or more of the additional services (specified for said district), the Council of the Merged Government shall reduce the rate of ad valorem taxation to a level commensurate with the kind, level, and type or character of services provided." The executive committee endorsed this recommendation at its meeting on February 8, 1972, and in due course it was adopted by the full commission.[7]

Obviously, this solution would not ensure the installation of street lights or sanitary sewers in those parts of the former city that did not have them. But there was some incentive for the proposed merged government to work toward that goal. If these facilities were not installed, the merged government, unlike the old city government, would suffer a substantial loss in property tax revenues. In any event the basic principle of relating property tax rates to services received had been extended to those who were included in the initial FUSD but who were not getting all services prescribed by the charter for that district.

At the final meeting of the Lexington-Fayette County Merger Commission, held on June 20, 1972, the formal agenda included minor technical changes in the language of various sections of the proposed charter that had been adopted earlier and giving second reading to several detailed substantive proposals that had been polished and tacitly approved beforehand. The only significant question raised that night centered on Carl Penske's abortive attempt to get the commission to reconsider its much-debated position on partisan versus nonpartisan elections.

It had been a long struggle. But after fifteen months of very hard work, the charter was ready to be submitted to the voters. Only one thing stood in the way of implementing the resolution to have the question of adopting the proposed charter placed on the ballot: following the unanimous passage of this resolution, the commission also voted to support the request of Robert Miller, a local attorney who was in the audience, to delay submitting the resolution to the county clerk for a period of three weeks to allow the public to inspect and comment upon the contents of the proposed charter. If, at the end of that time, the executive committee had not received any complaints that justified calling a special session of the full commission, the resolution to have the question of adopting the charter placed on the November 7, 1972, ballot would be implemented.[8]

8

~~~~~~

Shaping the Promerger Campaign

THE COMMISSION did not receive a single letter, telephone call, or personal contact protesting the wording or substance of the proposed charter during the three weeks allotted to public inspection following the June 20, 1972, meeting.[1] Even Robert Miller, the local attorney who had argued so strenuously for the delay, failed to communicate any displeasure with the document. Thus, the chairman of the commission filed the June 20 resolution along with a copy of the charter with the county clerk on July 17, 1972.[2]

There were still a few loose ends to be taken care of, including a pending appeal of the Fayette County Circuit Court's February 4, 1972, ruling that the enabling legislation under which the charter commission had operated was valid.[3] Nevertheless, the filing of the commission's resolution placed the merger question in the hands of the local electorate, even though the voters would not go to the polls for another three and one-half months.

The question of what to do about organizing voter support was first discussed in the spring of 1970 when the members of GO were preparing to initiate the petition drive to have a charter commission established. However, little serious interest was shown until early 1972. From that point on, it became an increasingly frequent topic of conversation among those who were involved in the merger effort.

As a participant in many of these informal discussions, the author discovered that there were essentially two points of view concerning campaign strategy. One preferred limiting the pro-merger campaign to a "low-profile" strategy aimed at simply making the contents of the proposed charter, perhaps along with some explanation of the rationale behind its various provisions, available to the voters. The other was in favor of a highly visible, precinct-by-precinct campaign to sell merger.

For the most part, those who advocated the low-profile approach seemed to base their arguments on two related assumptions. First, most voters would, or at least should, make up their minds on a question like merger after gathering and carefully examining all of the available evidence, including the contents of the proposed charter. ("Why," many of them would ask, "would it not be sufficient to publish the charter in the newspaper or put copies of the document on file in places like the public library?") Second, given an opportunity to read the charter and related documents, most voters would quickly agree that the merits of merger were self-evident and irrefutable.[4] (Another favorite question of the "low-profile" supporters was "Who could possibly be against merger?")

Most of the leading advocates of an all-out campaign to sell merger were campaign-hardened veterans of other political wars. Some had been candidates for political office; others had worked in various capacities in national, state, or local election contests. To them a merger referendum was merely another election. As such, they argued, it required a campaign similar to that conducted by any serious candidate for a major political office in the community. While none of these politically seasoned veterans seemed prepared to argue that this strategy would ensure victory at the polls, most of them felt that without a major campaign effort, merger was sure to be defeated.

Although I had never been directly involved in a political campaign up to that point, I found myself vigorously supporting the "hard-sell" approach throughout these informal discussions. I did so partly for emotional reasons. I simply could not commit time and energy to the Lexington merger effort while entertaining the notion of virtually abandoning the field to the opponents of merger during the campaign stage of the process. Having witnessed first-hand the campaign conducted by the antimerger forces in Augusta in 1971, I had some idea of how rough the competition could become during the final weeks preceding the vote.[5] And the specter of countering that kind of opposition by placing some copies of the proposed charter in the Lexington Public Library was scary indeed.

But there was more to it than this. I found it impossible as a political scientist to accept what appeared to be the underlying assumptions of those who preached the low-profile strategy. There is a very large body of empirical evidence concerning public opinion formation, and none of it supports the contention that most voters arrive at a decision on such issues as merger according to the tenets of what Walter Lippmann once described as the myth of the "Omnicompetent Citizen."[6] Even if one conceded that Lexington voters might turn out to be the exception to the rule, there was still the related assumption concerning the kind of conclusion they would reach after gathering and weighing all of the evidence. Certainly the record of voter reactions to merger proposals in other communities since World War II did not suggest that most voters would automatically conclude that the merits of merger were self-evident and irrefutable.

It was one thing to reject the assumptions of those who advocated the low-profile strategy. It was quite another matter to find sound, empirically based reasons for supporting the hard-sell approach. Once the problem was defined in these terms, it became necessary to ask the question: What kind of impact or benefit might one expect from such a campaign? In the absence of any systematic comparative studies of merger campaigns and their impact upon voter reactions, this was an exceedingly difficult question to answer.

One could turn to the widely accepted finding that campaigns serve more to activate and reinforce existing predispositions than as vehicles for converting voters from one position to another. Unfortunately, most of the hard evidence concerning this hypothesis is based on studies of presidential elections where factors such as party identification have traditionally provided most voters with a relatively stable and well defined set of predispositions. Given these predispositions, it may not be surprising that voters tend to engage in "selective perception" during presidential campaigns which, in turn, leads to a process of reinforcement of these predispositions rather than conversion.

The reinforcement hypothesis has also been confirmed in a number of other studies based on data drawn from nonpresidential elections. But in every case, the evidence is based on situations in which voters tended to have rather well defined and discernible predispositions before being subjected to a campaign. Thus Hyman and Sheatsley, in one of the very early experimental studies of the impact of "educational campaigns," found that their contrived campaign to win support for a proposal calling for the United States to make a large postwar reconstruction loan to England had a profound impact on those who were already "trustful" of England, but virtually no impact on those who were initially "distrustful" of England.[7]

The basic question, of course, was whether these widely accepted findings could be applied to a merger referendum. After all, the "reinforcement" hypothesis assumes the existence of a discernible set of predispositions toward some general object that can serve as a frame of reference for perceiving and evaluating information about more specific dimensions of that object. Did most voters have a discernible set of predispositions toward the general idea of merger that might guide their perceptions and evaluations of a specific plan or charter for implementing the idea?

At the outset of the Lexington merger effort, it was impossible to bring any hard evidence to bear on this crucial question. No survey data were available concerning the predispositions, if any, of Lexington voters toward the general idea of consolidating the city and county governments. And there was little evidence on the subject in the existing literature concerning other merger situations.[8]

In the absence of such information, it was necessary to consider the literature on the impact of campaign activities upon voter attitudes and behavior in other types of issue-oriented referenda. Again, there were no data with which to confirm the applicability of the findings drawn from this literature to merger referenda. But merger is essentially an issue-oriented question, and this seemed to suggest that it would be useful to consider the findings concerning voter reactions to other types of issue-specific referenda.[9]

If one accepted this argument, then one had also to accept the premise that issue-oriented referenda are *not* like most other elections, and that campaigns are therefore likely to play a different role from that suggested by the "reinforcement" hypothesis. The basic thrust of the findings on this point seemed to be that campaign activities before referenda play an important role in structuring voter attitudes and behavior. Operating without well-defined predispositions with which to perceive and evaluate the specific issue at hand, most voters become more dependent upon media and other types of campaign efforts for cues about what to do. In addition, they become less able to engage in the selective perception of those cues.

The idea that perhaps a merger referendum is more akin to other types of issue-oriented referenda than to the elections described in the literature supporting the reinforcement hypothesis was logically attractive and allowed one to support the wisdom of doing everything possible to create support for merger from scratch. It also provided a reasonable answer with which to counter the "low-profile" argument.

The ideal situation, however, seemed to be one in which the campaign strategy of the promerger forces could be directed primarily at reinforcing favorable predispositions of a *majority* of voters rather than trying to create favorable attitudes. But there seemed to be little point in trying to reinforce support for the idea of merger if only a small fraction of the voters had predispositions to lean in that direction. And if most voters had no discernible predispositions for or against merger, the antimerger forces would presumably have an equal shot at trying to structure voter attitudes and behavior during the campaign stage in the process.

It was with these points in mind that the author seized the opportunity to explore the general contours of the problem confronting the promerger forces in Lexington. In March 1971, shortly after the announcement had been made that a charter commission had been established, a random sample of Lexington-Fayette County adults was asked to respond to the following question: "Recently there has been talk about merging the City of Lexington and Fayette County into one government. Although the details have not been worked out yet, would you say that you would: Strongly Support, Support, Slightly Support, Slightly Oppose, Oppose, or Strongly Oppose the general idea of merger?"[10]

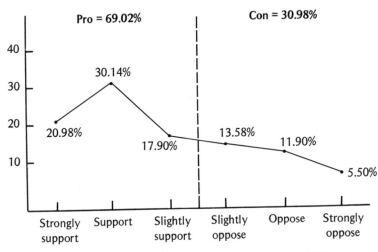

Figure 5. Attitudes toward Merger, March 1971

It was comforting to discover that over 95 percent of the respondents in this survey had an opinion on the subject even though
not a single line of the proposed charter had been written up to that
point. More comforting still, however, were the direction and intensity of the "predispositions" expressed by those who had an
opinion on the subject. As noted in Figure 5, over 69 percent were
favorably disposed toward the idea of merger. Moreover, the average strength or intensity of feelings was clearly higher among those
who favored the idea.

It was not a highly sophisticated study of voter predispositions,
but it did suggest that it would be folly for the promerger forces to
write off the "reinforcement" hypothesis if and when the question
of merger ever came to a vote in Lexington. Assuming the charter
commission did nothing to stir up major opposition during the
charter preparation stage, the findings of this preliminary study suggested that the promerger forces would be in a very favorable position to mount an all-out campaign to reinforce voter support. The
opposition forces would have to deal with the very difficult task of
converting voters.

The conclusions drawn from this March 1971 probe of voter
attitudes were underscored several months later when the author

obtained a copy of another survey of voter opinions on merger. This survey of *city* voters had been ordered by the Underwood majority on the Lexington City Commission and was conducted by John F. Kraft, a well-known polling firm, early in August 1971.

Some observers speculated that Underwood had ordered the survey in order to see whether it would make sense for him to build his campaign for the office of mayor in the fall of 1971 around the merger issue. Whatever his motives, Underwood never released the results of the poll to the public. Nor did he mention the merger issue during his unsuccessful primary campaign in September.

In view of Underwood's opposition to the merger idea, it was easy to understand why he tried to conceal the results of the Kraft poll. Over 80 percent of all *city* voters in the sample held an opinion on the subject of merger, and over 80 percent of those who held an opinion said they would support "merging the county and city governments" if the election were held in August 1971.[11]

The Kraft poll also contained some interesting findings for those who worried about trying to explain the advantages of merger to city voters who already had most urban services.[12] For example, the Kraft data indicated that almost half of all city voters felt that merger would result in "better" services for city residents. A similar percentage felt that their services would remain the "same" under merger. Only a small percentage felt that their services would be "worse" if merger took place.

Taken together, the March 1971 poll conducted by the author and the August 1971 poll of city voters by Kraft suggested that a substantial majority of voters held favorable predispositions toward merger. The numbers seemed to be there to win a merger referendum if: (a) the charter commission could produce a charter that would command the support of most opinion leaders and groups in the community; and (b) the promerger forces were prepared to wage an all-out effort to sustain and reinforce the apparent promerger inclinations of most voters.

As often happens, the decision concerning the type of campaign that was most desirable was made by a few individuals. In the Lexington case, it was Mayor Foster Pettit who seized the initiative. Early in May 1972 Pettit asked the chairman of the charter commission to meet with him to discuss organizing a campaign on behalf of merger. The only other person invited to the meeting was Steve Driesler, the mayor's administrative assistant, who had developed something of a reputation as a political campaign organizer in the community. These three were in agreement on the question of strategy. Pettit supported the hard-sell approach as an experienced politician. Driesler shared the view that a merger referendum was in the final analysis an election that would be won by the side that mounted the best campaign. And the author openly and actively supported the hard-sell approach for the reasons outlined above.

Various topics were explored during this initial meeting. Views were exchanged concerning the need for an all-out campaign effort, the basic purposes of such an endeavor, and the kinds of tactics and finances it would take to do the job. Most of the meeting, however, was devoted to the question of how to set the campaign in motion.

Before the meeting came to an end, it was decided that it would not be wise to have the charter commission serve as the organizational vehicle for waging the promerger campaign. It would not be very useful, it was argued, to have it appear that the only group in town promoting the adoption of the charter was the group that wrote it. This did not mean that individuals who served on the charter commission would be discouraged from participating in the campaign. It merely meant that the Lexington-Fayette County Merger Commission would not be used as a campaign organization or even as the nucleus of such an organization. Clearly then it would be necessary to create a separate citizens' body to organize and conduct the promerger campaign. Ideally such an organization ought to be composed of respected and well-known citizens from all segments of the community, but not highly visible participants in the merger effort up to that point.

Support for these ideas was sought at a series of meetings called by Mayor Pettit during May and June 1972. The participants at these meetings represented the political and civic leadership of the community. Among those drawn from the political world were County Judge Robert Stephens; County Commissioners Jack Lynch and Doc Ferrell; City Commissioners J. Farra Van Meter, Bill Hoskins, and Scott Yellman; State Senator Michael Moloney (D); and State Representatives Joe Graves (R), Larry Hopkins (R), and William Kenton (D). Also participating was former State Representative Bart Peak, who had coauthored the original enabling legislation upon which the whole Lexington merger effort was based.

Another dozen or more people were drawn from the leadership ranks of such civic groups as the Chamber of Commerce, the Rotary Club, the Jaycees, and the League of Women Voters. Representatives from the black community, environmental groups, the religious community, and various segments of the business community also accepted invitations to attend.

These civic and political leaders quickly agreed that a separate "citizens for merger" organization would be needed to wage the campaign. They also agreed that such an organization needed to be as broadly based as possible, yet composed of individuals who had not been visibly associated with the work of the charter commission.

Another principle emerged from these meetings—one that may seem a bit strange at first glance. It was decided, with the support of the political leaders attending these planning sessions, that the official roster of the citizens' group that was to be formed should not include the names of any elected political leaders. Most of them eventually worked very hard for merger. Some were even drafted to be very visible spokesmen for the cause before the campaign was over. But at this very early stage in the campaign process most of those involved agreed that it would be better if their names did not appear on the list of members of the citizens' group.

Cynics may interpret this as simply another example of how politicians manage to "eat their cake and have it too" in touchy situations. If things went well they could jump in and grab some of the credit whether their name was on the letterhead of the campaign group or not. If things began to turn sour for the promerger forces they could lie low and say they were never formally allied with the cause.

While this line of argument may have crossed the minds of the political leaders involved, it should also be noted that the civic leaders eagerly accepted the idea of not putting politicians on the membership list of the campaign organization. For some of these civic leaders, the goal seemed to be one of making the merger campaign more like a United Fund drive than an overtly political effort. For others, including the author, there seemed to be some virtue in testing the political popularity of these elected officials before using them as spokesmen for merger. After all, none of the county Fiscal Court members had faced the electorate since 1969, and the mayor and his City Commission were pushing for a one-half of one percent increase in the city wage tax that could easily end their honeymoon with the voters before the November 1972 election.

Once these basic principles were worked out, the civic and political leaders tackled the job of finding someone to head the proposed "citizens for merger" organization. The group soon agreed to ask Penrose Ecton to serve as the chairman of what was to become known as the Committee to Insure Good Government (CIGG).[13] Everyone agreed that "Penny" would be an ideal choice. He was a longtime resident of Lexington and a respected civic leader who had been active in scores of civic, professional, business, and church groups. Indeed it was hard to name very many community groups or organizations that Ecton had not served in a leadership capacity at one time or another.

Ecton was also a world traveler who excited people's envy. He had sailed the Caribbean and paddled a dugout canoe up jungle rivers in South America. Everyone, it seemed, knew of his exploits and recognized him as one of the most popular and entertaining after-dinner speakers in town. The fact that he could also give eloquent testimony about his experiences as the first city manager of Baton Rouge, Louisiana, after that community adopted a consolidation proposal back in the 1940s was just so much icing on the cake.

Once Ecton agreed to serve, Harry Sykes was named as vice-chairman and Jerry Smith as treasurer of the CIGG. Both of these men had impressive credentials and were important additions to the team. Sykes was not only an important leader in the black community, he was the acting city manager of Lexington, a former city commissioner, and a former Harlem Globetrotter. (In a town with a strong basketball tradition, this last item was of more than passing consequence.)

Jerry Smith was an executive with the local private water company and a well-known fund raiser for such causes as the United Fund. Jerry was the only charter commission member to be listed among the forty names on the CIGG letterhead. But he had the experience, contacts, and image that most civic and political leaders felt would be needed to raise money for the campaign.

All of these designated officers served as unpaid volunteers throughout the campaign. However, it was obvious from the outset that it would be necessary to have someone with experience in running a major community-wide campaign at the helm on a full-time basis. In order to fill this need, Mayor Pettit agreed to release Steven Driesler from his duties as administrative assistant to the mayor so that he might serve as the full-time, paid executive director of the CIGG. Driesler was taken off the city payroll in July 1972 to assume his new duties.

Although Driesler was only twenty-four years old at the time and about to enter his final year in law school in the fall of 1972, he had put together an impressive record as a campaigner. Starting as a teenager, he had helped organize a statewide group known as Teen-age Republicans. From there he moved on to serve as a campaign manager for Larry Hopkins in his unsuccessful 1969 county commission race. Two years later he was a key campaign organizer for Hopkins and Joe Graves during their successful bids for seats in the Kentucky General Assembly from Fayette County. Since both candidates won as Republicans in districts that were predominantly Democratic, Driesler was able to command considerable attention as a campaign manager. Despite his obvious ties to Republican contenders, he had maintained contact with people outside his own party. The mere fact that he was the administrative assistant to a mayor who had once held a seat as a Democrat in the General Assembly provided some indication that Driesler could put aside partisan considerations for the right cause.[14]

Some of the other thirty-six members listed on the letterhead had participated in the formation of the group; others had been asked to serve by those who met with the mayor to establish the campaign organization. Taken together, the officers and members of the CIGG included registered Democrats and Republicans, city and county residents, blacks, females, religious leaders, university people, homebuilders, realtors, IBM employees, civil servants, Chamber of Commerce members, members of the League of Women Voters, and members of various civic clubs.

The members of the CIGG advised Ecton and Driesler on matters of basic policy through a series of committees. However, considerable discretion was left to these two men, and Penrose Ecton left his executive director virtually free to conduct the actual campaign. Driesler also had a free hand in selecting his staff, assigning duties to campaign workers, and running the campaign headquarters.

All political campaigns depend heavily on volunteers, and the promerger campaign in Lexington was no exception. In fact, other than Driesler and one assistant, Dianne Smith, the only workers who were paid by the CIGG were the handful of people who helped conduct interviews for a public opinion survey done in August 1972 and those who helped with the keypunching chores for a computerized mailing system. All other workers at the campaign headquarters and in the field were strictly volunteers.

It is impossible to put a dollar figure on the contribution of the scores of volunteers who labored for the promerger campaign. It is equally impossible to calculate the value of the many in-kind contributions ranging from the loan of a three-room office suite for a campaign headquarters by a local realtor to the free use of keypunch machines during nonbusiness hours at a local computer service firm. Without such contributions it would have been impossible for the promerger forces to conduct the kind of campaign they had in mind on a cash budget that amounted to less than $50,000. In the view of many local political observers, this was a "bare bones" cash budget for waging a community-wide campaign of the magnitude contemplated by the promerger forces.[15]

It took some effort to raise this sum. Kentucky law forbids business corporations to make political contributions, and the CIGG's request to have itself declared a charitable organization was turned down by both the state authorities and the federal Internal Revenue Service. All donations would have to come from individuals or groups that were not incorporated under Kentucky law to do business. And there was even some question about whether certain groups might risk their federal tax-exempt status by donating funds to the CIGG.

Perhaps the greatest problem, however, was that there were few incentives for anyone to risk getting caught in the many gray areas in the tax laws. If merger won, there were no identifiable political debts to be called in by anyone who contributed. (How do you remind a "cause" that you gave when the balloting is over?) In short, the CIGG was forced by both law and circumstance to pitch its appeal for dollars in purely altruistic, "let's help the community" terms.

This appeal was effective. Hundreds of small donations were solicited and received. Several civic groups came forward with substantial checks.[16] The mayor personally donated the money to pay the salaries of the CIGG staff for the first month of its operation. And one anonymous personal contribution of $5,000 came in to bolster both the spirits and the treasury of the promerger campaign forces.

The biggest single chunk of money, however, was raised by selling tickets to a fund-raising dinner and rally held in the clubhouse of the Red Mile racetrack on October 10. Over $28,000 was netted by selling $25 tickets to this affair, which featured Mayor Beverly Briley of Nashville as the main speaker. Tickets were sold to individuals and businesses either singly or in blocks.[17] (Purchasing a ticket to a dinner did not violate the legal prohibition against corporations making campaign contributions.)

Fund raising, of course, was a constant activity throughout the entire campaign. Indeed, it continued after the election was over so that the CIGG could pay several relatively small debts. But sufficient amounts of money and pledges began to come in by late August to allow the CIGG to proceed with its plan to wage an all-out, precinct-by-precinct campaign on behalf of merger.

Two things became apparent as the leaders of the CIGG began to think about actually launching the campaign in the fall of 1972. One was that a merger referendum was not going to be just another election. There would be no candidate or party label around which this campaign could be organized. It would be purely a matter of trying to sell an idea. Second, the concept of merger could not be treated as essentially a single issue like fluoridation or a school bond proposal. The proposed charter raised a host of questions ranging from the pension benefits of government employees to the distribution of the costs and benefits of local services among various segments of the community. In short, many specific issues were raised by the forty-page charter for people to react to regardless of their feelings toward the general idea of merger.

It was therefore decided that the first major expenditure of time and money by the CIGG ought to be for an in-depth study of voter attitudes toward as many aspects of the merger question as possible.[18] Polls and surveys, of course, are commonly used in contemporary election campaigns. But the leaders of the Lexington promerger campaign had in mind a survey that would go beyond the traditional name-recognition and issue-identification poll used by most candidates. Moreover, they wanted something more than just another standard poll of how voters felt about merger.

The study, which was directed by the author, involved face-to-face interviews lasting approximately twenty to thirty minutes with 350 randomly selected registered voters in Lexington and Fayette County. All interviews were conducted by a team of workers trained by the author and Driesler.[19] Telephone calls were made on a random basis after each interviewer turned in his or her questionnaires in order to insure the integrity of the fieldwork.

Most of the interviews were completed during the last two weeks of August, though a few had to be done in early September. After eliminating those respondents who no longer resided at the address given on the voter registration list, and those who were either chronically not at home or refused to be interviewed, the number of completed interviews stood at 285.

The first thing learned after the results of the survey were coded and tabulated was that little had changed in terms of the basic distribution of voter attitudes toward merger since the author conducted the March 1971 poll. An overwhelming majority of Lexington and Fayette County respondents still held an opinion on merger (89.4 percent in the August 1972 survey compared with

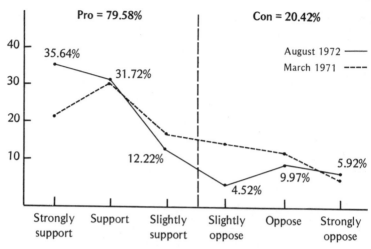

Figure 6. Attitudes toward Merger,
August 1972 versus March 1971

95.8 percent in the March 1971 poll). More important, a very substantial percentage of all *opinion-holders* still said they were for merger (79.6 percent in August 1972 versus 69.0 percent in the 1971 poll).

In fact, the only really significant difference between the findings of the March 1971 and the August 1972 polls on this point seemed to be that in the process of picking up some strength on the *pro* side of the ledger the promerger forces had also improved their position in terms of intensity of feelings. However, the gains in intensity of feelings among those who supported merger were not so great as might be expected by merely glancing at the trend lines shown in Figure 6. If one computes the average intensity score for supporters and opponents in the two polls, it becomes clear that both sides gained ground in the time between the 1971 and 1972 polls. The proponents were still ahead in intensity of feelings, but the gap between the average intensity scores had narrowed from .64 in 1971 to .23 in August of 1972.[20]

Opinions had hardened a bit since the 1971 poll on both sides of the issue. Nevertheless, the overall pattern found in the August 1972 survey clearly suggested that it would be foolish for the pro-

Table 2. RELCI Orientations and Attitudes toward Merger
(Tau-B = −.129; N = 253)

RELCI	*Promerger*	*Antimerger*	*N*
Procity	69.7%	30.3%	76
Indifferent	82.4	17.6	153
Procounty	83.3	16.7	24

merger forces to run a campaign aimed primarily at converting those who opposed the idea, or winning the support of those who remained undecided. Victory, it seemed, could best be ensured by a campaign to sustain and reinforce the margin of support for merger.

Some of the other data generated by the August 1972 survey now began to take on special meaning. Intuitive feelings were expressed about which aspects of the merger question ought to be stressed in order to reinforce voter support for merger. Some of these "gut" feelings squared with the findings of the August 1972 survey, but others had to be rejected or modified in light of the survey data received.

For example, some members of the promerger campaign insisted that there were considerable social differences between city and county residents, and that the battle over merger would be won or lost on the basis of the time and effort promerger forces devoted to blunting this problem. According to the data generated by the August 1972 survey, however, there seemed little need to worry about trying to create, convert, or reinforce voter attitudes toward merger on the basis of any social-distance considerations.

Almost two-thirds of our respondents failed to see any differences between the way in which city and county residents lived and conducted themselves as measured by the Relative Community Identification Index (RELCI).[21] Moreover, the relationship between respondent RELCI scores and attitudes toward merger was a very weak −.129 (Tau-B). As can be seen in Table 2, the only group of respondents displaying any noteworthy opposition to merger were those who both perceived sharp differences between city and county dwellers and identified more positively with city dwellers on the RELCI index. But even these seventy-six respondents supported merger better than two to one.

These findings squared with those of the author in his study of fringe voters in Lexington during the 1969 annexation controversy. And they also matched the findings of the author's study of attitudes among fringe voters just prior to the 1971 referendum on merger in Augusta, Georgia. Neither of these previous studies had indicated that the social-distance argument, as measured by the RELCI index, was a dimension along which very many voters were organizing their reactions to proposals calling for the political integration of local governments.[22]

The major contribution of the August 1972 survey, however, was that for the first time the RELCI index had been administered to a sample that included both city and fringe voters. The fact that the very weak correlation between respondent scores on the RELCI index and voter attitudes toward merger remained virtually unchanged when controls for place of residence (city or county) were introduced merely strengthened the case for not focusing time and attention on the social-distance argument. In fact, these relationships were so low that it seemed foolish for the promerger forces even to worry about any move on the part of the opposition to enlist city and county voters against merger in terms of their social differences. The lack of correspondence between the boundaries of "social worlds" and the political boundary between the old city and county governments seemed to have had its effect.

Two other highly generalized sets of "gut" feelings, however, seemed to be borne out by the findings of the August 1972 survey: the belief that voters would react to merger on the basis of their perceptions of how it might affect their taxes and services, and the belief that voters would react primarily to perceptions of how the proposed charter might alter the basic structure and operation of local government. The former, of course, represented the tax-benefit argument discussed earlier. The latter reflected a concern about what has been discussed as the regime-government argument.

The relationship between the measure of tax-benefit orientations and attitudes toward merger among Lexington and Fayette County voters was .522 (Tau-B).[23] And the relationship between our measure of regime-government orientations known as the Relative

Regime Trust (RELRT) and voter attitudes toward merger was .492 (Tau-B).[24] When these scores were compared to the −.129 Tau-B obtained when voter scores on the RELCI index were correlated with voter attitudes toward merger, there was little doubt that the tax-benefit and regime-government dimensions of the problem ought to receive some attention (see Tables 3 and 4).

Furthermore, neither the tax-benefit nor the regime-government findings seemed to be affected in any substantial way when the relationships were controlled for such factors as age, sex, income, occupation, education, or city versus county residence. More important, an analysis of the relative impact of the social-distance, regime-government, and tax-benefit orientations upon voter attitudes toward merger revealed a pattern that was virtually identical to that found among fringe voters in the 1971 Augusta, Georgia, merger situation.[25] This pattern, moreover, was maintained even though the 1972 Lexington survey included both city and fringe respondents. No matter how one interpreted the findings of the August 1972 Lexington survey, it seemed clear that the quest for voter support in November would revolve around basically two sets of arguments—tax-benefit and regime-government.

Useful as these findings were in helping the promerger forces decide where to cast their nets, they provided little insight into the kinds of specific concerns that might be prompting voters to organize their attitudes toward merger around these two basic sets of sociopolitical orientations. Although political intuition had to be used heavily at this point, the survey did provide some additional information to help guide the campaign leaders. These additional bits of information were obtained from an analysis of responses given to a series of rather specific questions tied to particular situations in the Lexington setting, and from a review of the responses obtained on an open-ended question asking respondents why they felt as they did about merger.

For example, it was discovered that 56.8 percent of our respondents felt that massive annexation of all built-up county areas by the city of Lexington would be a "worse idea than merger." Another 23.8 percent said it would make little difference whether we had

Table 3. Tax-Benefit Orientations and Attitudes toward Merger
(Tau-B = .522; N = 229)

Tax-Benefit Orientation	Promerger	Antimerger	N
More benefits	97.7%	2.3%	128
Same benefits	70.9	29.1	79
Fewer benefits	22.7	77.3	22

merger or annexation. And only 19.4 percent favored annexation over merger. As might have been expected, there was a very strong relationship between voter attitudes toward annexation and feelings about merger.

But the really important point seemed to be that when the responses of county residents threatened by annexation were examined, the message remained the same. Most county voters who lived in the areas open to massive annexation in 1975 and 1980 saw merger as a better option than annexation, and most of them responded positively to the question of merger.

Although this same basic relationship was obtained when the data for city residents were examined, it was decided that, for the purposes of a reinforcement campaign, major attention should be given to the annexation "threat" when it came to appealing to those county voters who lived in the areas affected by the court order handed down during the Underwood administration. Furthermore, it was decided to treat the annexation question as essentially a tax-benefit issue, even though one could argue that being annexed by a city also carries certain regime-government implications.[26]

On the more clearly regime-government side of the ledger, the August 1972 survey yielded some valuable information also. Regime-government orientations can revolve around a wide variety of structural, procedural, and political-leadership questions. The August survey tried to tap some of the more potentially relevant aspects of these specific regime-government questions.

One question was designed to measure the extent to which voters could relate to the regime-government changes likely to occur if merger failed and the state legislature came under pressure to re-

Table 4. RELRT Orientations and Attitudes toward Merger
(Tau-B = .492; N = 252)

RELRT	Promerger	Antimerger	N
Trust proposed gov't more	97.5%	2.5%	81
See no difference	83.0	17.0	135
Trust existing gov't more	19.4	80.6	36

classify Lexington as a first-class city under the provisions of the state constitution.

No one assumed that most voters could identify all specific features of first-class city government, or the "Louisville form" as it was often called. But it was assumed that perhaps most voters could relate to a question about whether they might prefer the Louisville system in general over the proposed merger. There was a risk, of course, that in trying to measure this reaction we would really get a measure of the well-known antipathy between Lexingtonians and Louisvillians. But in designing the question we did try to focus attention on the issue of perceived differences in government forms.

To judge by the responses obtained in the August survey, it seemed rather clear that the "first-class city" question was not likely to become a major issue in the merger campaign. Over half of all respondents said that they could not answer the question on whether the "Louisville form of government" would be "better," "worse," or would make "little difference" for the Lexington community. Another 15 percent said it would make "no difference" to them if Lexington became a first-class city under the Louisville form of government. Only 5.5 percent said it would be "better" for the community to have the Louisville form, while 28.7 percent said that they thought it would be "worse" than merger.

Despite the obvious implications of these findings, the leaders of the CIGG agreed that they could not totally ignore the first-class city issue. Some felt that it was still likely to become an important and salient factor during the campaign. The rumblings from at least one known opponent to merger, William Jacobs, gave some reason to suspect that the opposition might attempt to make this a major plank in the antimerger platform.

Thus the leaders of the CIGG agreed to deal with this question in terms of the theme—"Change is in the air." Emphasis was placed on trying to point out to city voters in particular that the status quo was not a viable option since their form of government would almost certainly change even if merger was defeated. This, of course, fit beautifully into the decision to show fringe voters that annexation made it unrealistic to think about merger versus the status quo.

There were, however, several other aspects of the regime-government argument that were probed by the August 1972 survey. One involved the question of how voters felt about the performance of the two leading political figures associated with the merger effort —Mayor Foster Pettit and County Judge Robert Stephens. It was hoped that voter responses to this kind of question would not only shed some light on the extent to which voters might be organizing their regime-government orientations around their feelings toward these political incumbents, but also help the leaders of the pro-merger campaign decide whether or not to encourage these political leaders to become major spokesmen for the cause.

The results of the survey were most encouraging on both counts. They suggested that it would be foolish to ignore the possible impact of the political incumbency aspect of regime-government orientations upon voter attitudes toward merger, and indeed they seemed to make it almost imperative that the promerger forces use these two particular political leaders to promote the cause of merger. The data presented in Table 5 could be construed in no other way. Over 90 percent of all voters who held an opinion on merger also rated the job performance of these two political leaders. And over 60 percent of these voters thought Pettit and Stephens were doing a better than average job. Furthermore, there was no major crumbling of support for merger except among the very small number of voters who felt these incumbents were doing a "very poor" job.

Regime-government orientations are not always structured

Table 5. Support for Merger by Voter Ratings
of Pettit and Stephens

Pettit (N = 236)			*Stephens (N = 229)*		
Performance Rating		Pro-merger	Performance Rating		Pro-merger
Superior	13.1%	87.1%	Superior	12.7%	86.2%
Good	49.6	84.6	Good	50.7	85.3
Average	28.4	73.1	Average	32.3	71.6
Rather poor	6.4	80.0	Rather poor	3.5	62.5
Very poor	2.5	33.3	Very poor	0.8	00.0

around public perceptions of the occupants of particular public offices. They can also revolve around perceptions and feelings concerning various institutions and processes that make up a particular political system. It seemed important, therefore, for the leaders of the Lexington promerger campaign to find out whether there were any particular institutional or procedural dimensions along which local voters were organizing their more generalized regime-government attitudes toward merger.

The big problem was deciding which of the many possible institutional and procedural questions raised by the proposed charter ought to be examined. The proposed questionnaire for the August 1972 survey was already quite long, and the inclusion of too many items makes a survey instrument unwieldy.

After considerable thought, it was decided that space would allow us to focus on only one specific institutional-procedural question—representation. Of all the institutional-procedural changes called for in the proposed charter, the system of representation was clearly the most dramatic. The proposed charter, it should be recalled, specified a system of electing twelve of the fifteen members of the Urban County Council by districts. Clearly this emphasis upon district representation marked a dramatic departure from tradition in the community.

Since no one really knew how local voters might react to this idea, it was interesting to discover that over 70 percent of *all* respondents for the August 1972 survey said that they thought district representation was a better idea than strictly at-large representation. When those who said they had no opinion on the subject were dropped from consideration, support for district representation rose to over 85 percent. More important, as shown in Table 6, over 84 percent of those who thought district representation was a "better idea" also supported merger.

This finding seemed to confirm the suspicion of many who worked on the merger charter that district representation might be a major asset to the cause of winning voter support. It also suggested that district representation could be made a key element in the campaign to reinforce the positive attitudes toward merger displayed by a sizable majority of voters.

Before leaving this subject, it should also be noted that the relationship shown in Table 6 was even stronger among black respondents. Although the number of black respondents in the sample was very small, it was comforting to discover that the data seemed to confirm what many black participants in the Lexington merger process had been saying all along—that the quest for black support would come down to the question of district representation.[27] All that remained, it seemed, was for the leaders of the promerger campaign to devise a way to keep hammering home the fact that blacks could not expect to get district representation by supporting the status quo or by hoping for Lexington to be reclassified as a first-class city.

Finally, all of these findings of the August 1972 survey seemed to be reinforced and confirmed by the results of the open-ended question on why respondents felt the way they did about merger. Although relatively few respondents were willing or able to spell out their specific reasons for supporting or opposing merger, the kinds of responses obtained were quite consistent with what has been reported thus far.

The most frequently mentioned reasons for supporting merger could be classified as tax-benefit arguments. Some respondents said that merger would be "more efficient and economical." Others saw it as a way to "put an end to the duplication and waste" of the present system. And still others felt that services would improve,

Table 6. Attitudes toward Merger by Opinions
on Representation

Representation Preferred	Promerger	Antimerger	N
District	84.2%	15.8%	203
At-large or no preference*	57.1	42.9	35

*These two categories combined because of small N.

especially in the areas of police and fire protection, if the "city-county boundary" could be erased. Next in line were the essentially regime-government arguments. Terms like "fairer," "more open," and "more representative" were used to describe the advantages of merger.

A similar pattern was found among those who articulated reasons for opposing merger. Under the heading of tax-benefit concerns, one could find such statements as: "It will cost too much"; "Taxes will go up"; "We won't get anything out of it"; and "The county (or city) does a good enough job of providing services now." And displaying regime-government concerns, opponents felt: "Merger is too complicated to work"; "Merger will give too much power to local officials"; and "I don't like Pettit or the other politicians who are behind the whole idea."

In sum, responses to the open-ended question seemed to point in the same direction as the other responses obtained by the survey. Most voters seemed to be organizing their attitudes toward merger around economic (tax-benefit) or regime-government considerations. Few voters were able to perceive sharp differences between city and county residents in terms of social distance, and most of those who did seemed prepared to abandon these opinions when they came into conflict with economic or regime-government orientations.

All that remained to be done was to translate these findings and the interpretations placed upon them by the leaders of the CIGG into a campaign that could be taken to the voters.

9

~~~~~~

Seeking Voter Support

THERE WERE really two promerger campaigns run by the CIGG. One was aimed primarily at organized groups and what might be called the very attentive public. The other was designed to reach the large mass of voters who were not very likely to read the charter, attend workshops or meetings to hear detailed explanations of the charter, or read long stories or editorials concerning merger in the press. Both campaigns, however, were built around the findings of the August 1972 survey.

Several techniques were used in the attempt to reach members of the attentive publics in the community. A speakers' bureau was set up to handle the scores of speeches and presentations requested by various civic, religious, educational, and neighborhood groups during the fall of 1972. Most of these speaking engagements were handled by the most visible proponents of merger—Mayor Pettit, Judge Stephens, Penrose Ecton, and the author.

For the most part the format of these speaking engagements allowed time for a reasonably detailed presentation followed by a question-and-answer period. This meant that the spokesmen for merger had to be thoroughly familiar with the contents of the proposed charter and the rationale behind its various provisions. There was no way one could predict what kinds of very detailed questions some of these audiences would ask.

Nevertheless, all members of the speakers' bureau were asked to stress at least four points during their presentations before groups. Two of these were couched in essentially tax-benefit terms, the other two focused upon regime-government arguments. These points were outlined in both the "sample speech" and the visual aid materials supplied to each speaker by the CIGG.

Speakers were urged to open their presentations by asking the question Why merger? If possible, they were to refer to a map that had been supplied showing the "crazy" city-county boundary. The author preferred to refer to the map as "our civic Rorschach test" and others began to follow suit. The point to be made, however, was that this boundary was not only visually and logically absurd— it stood in the way of providing quality services to both city and county residents.

Although most of the speakers had their own favorite stories to relate, examples were given to each member of the speakers' bureau to illustrate the tax-benefit implications of this point. The map clearly showed how many city fire stations were virtually surrounded by county territory and vice-versa, and examples were given to illustrate how jurisdictional conflicts between city and county police and fire units had cost citizens valuable time, money, and service. It was pointed out that citizens could tell where that "crazy" city-county line went by observing where the weed cutters and pot-hole fillers for the city or county governments stopped and moved on to seek some other patch of weeds or section of road within their respective jurisdictions.

Speakers were free to inject any other economy-efficiency arguments they wished. While some people in the community can be moved by profound discussions of the economies of scale to be obtained by such moves as centralized purchasing, the materials provided by the CIGG for group consumption strongly urged speakers to hammer home the point that the elimination of the boundary between the city and county would be a major move toward "squeezing more out of each tax dollar spent" for such community-wide services as police and fire protection, streets, and roads.

Speakers were also urged to follow up this tax-benefit theme by noting that most of the built-up areas outside the city were subject to annexation by the city under the 1975/1980 schedule handed down by the local courts during the Underwood regime. They were also urged to note that, while a 1969 amendment to the state constitution allowed local governments to set up a variable property tax rate based on services received, no unit of local government had yet exercised this option. Thus, under the prevailing norms, being annexed by the city would result in an immediate 67 percent increase in property tax rates with no guarantee of when the city would provide the additional services that supposedly went with being in the city. Under merger, these county residents would not have their property tax rate raised until they received additional services.

On the regime-government topic, speakers were asked to emphasize the advantages of district representation over the strictly at-large system employed by the existing city and county governments. And they were instructed to point out that city residents would not be able to get district representation under existing state laws if Lexington became a first-class city.

Speakers were also asked to point out other possible implications of a merger defeat. For example, under the provisions of KRS 67A, the people of Lexington and Fayette County would not be able to consider merger again unless the exclusion of counties with first-class cities in the law should be changed. In addition, if Lexington became a first-class city before merger could be effected, it would mean that all local elections would probably have to be held on a partisan ballot.

The "chicken and peas circuit" provided a way to present the case for merger to many very attentive people. But it could not ensure that the promerger forces were getting their message across to the attentive publics which might not be active in organized groups. The CIGG therefore decided to pursue two other approaches to the problem of reaching the attentive voter.

One approach involved the scheduling of over 150 coffees in various precincts throughout the Lexington and Fayette County area.[1] No one in the CIGG expected that these coffees would turn out large numbers of voters. The goal was to get enough people to attend each coffee so that every precinct would have an indigenous set of committed and well-informed opinion leaders speaking out among their friends and neighbors for merger. The CIGG decided to mail the invitations for these coffees to every registered voter in the immediate area of the host, notifying them of the time, place, and hour of the event.[2] This relieved the host of the chore of getting a crowd to the coffee, and it also put the idea of merger before many voters who fell into the "mass electorate" category.

Audiences at these coffees ranged between two (the host and hostess) and thirty people. On the average, one talked with eight to ten people. Almost without exception those who attended these coffees were promerger and eager to find out more about the details of the proposed charter. Copies of the charter were made available to all who came. Speakers were asked to focus on the same key points used by those who appeared before organized groups. And they were urged to use the maps showing the "crazy" city-county boundary, the areas to be affected by the annexation order of the local court, and the boundaries of the twelve single-member districts that would be created under the merger charter.

Efforts were also made to explain these same basic points in some detail through the media. Spokesmen for merger were assigned to appear on every radio and television public service program that would have them, even though these programs tended to be aired at rather unusual hours. It was difficult to get very excited about appearing on a public service TV program to be seen at two o'clock Sunday afternoon opposite a major professional football game on another channel. But there were those who listened to or viewed this type of program on radio and television. Most of them, it was assumed, could be counted among the more attentive voters.

The CIGG tried to overcome the problems associated with using public service programs to reach the attentive public. An agreement was reached with two of the three local TV stations to purchase a half-hour of air time for a simultaneous broadcast featuring Steve Driesler and the author, who would answer specific questions phoned in by viewers during the show. It was expensive, but it seemed the only way to avoid the pitfalls of public service programs.

Newspaper ads were run to notify viewers of the program, which was scheduled to be aired at 7 P.M. on Friday, November 3, 1972. The telephone number for the call-in program was listed, and voters were urged to watch either channel 18 (NBC) or channel 27 (CBS).

If the decision had had to be made again, there probably would have been no paid, televised call-in program. It was not that viewers failed to call in questions, or that anyone complained about not receiving a full and straightforward answer from Driesler or Lyons. Nor were there any major problems with the telephones. The problem was that too many people tried to call in questions only to find all twelve lines busy. This led to complaints from some viewers that the program was rigged—that all those people seen on TV answering phones were just pretending, or that the questions answered on the air were written by the CIGG prior to broadcast time.

Finally, the CIGG tried to carry its message to the attentive public through the local press. Most of the basic points being made by the CIGG had been touched upon in editorials, cartoons, and news stories, and in published reports of interviews with various promerger leaders. But the CIGG also got a chance to repeat these basic themes without having them filtered through a reporter when the author was asked to write a series of five front-page editorials for the *Lexington Leader*. The series was published during the last full week before the election.[3]

There was nothing unusual about the fact that the CIGG tried to reach various segments of the attentive public in Lexington. The number of speeches, coffees, and public service presentations used in the Lexington setting may have been larger than in other promerger campaigns. And the role played by the findings of the August 1972 survey in helping the leaders of the CIGG decide how to structure their key arguments may have been rather atypical. But according to the scattered written references concerning other merger campaigns, the essential features of the Lexington campaign at this level seemed to be consistent with what had been done by the proponents of merger in other settings.

It was at the level of appealing to the mass electorate that the strategy and tactics of the Lexington promerger forces began to part company with most other promerger campaigns. Every major technique known to experts in mass communications was used to implement the basic reinforcement strategy of the CIGG at this level. Radio and television commercials were produced and aired on every station in town. Newspaper ads, varying in size from large, quarter-page spreads to tiny spots in the classified pages, were run with increasing frequency in both local newspapers as the November election drew near. And an elaborate, computerized mailing system was set up to allow selective messages to be sent to various segments of the local electorate.

The television commercials that were run on all three local channels were typical of the kinds of messages put out via the electronic media. Three thirty-second spots were prepared, featuring Mayor Pettit, County Judge Stephens, and Penrose Ecton. Each of these individuals focused on one of three basic themes—the boundary problem, district representation, and the "you can't afford to bet on the status quo" idea. These same points were repeated in a series of ten-second commercials made by the author.

The newspaper advertising campaign, on the other hand, focused primarily on the tax-benefit theme. One of the basic series of newspaper ads began with a black-on-white map of the city of Lexington, in which the contours of the city really did look very much like a Rorschach ink blot test. The map was run under the caption "Does This Make Any Sense to YOU?" Subsequent versions of the ad kept getting larger and began to include references to the waste, inefficiency, and jurisdictional conflicts caused by the crazy, patchwork boundary between the city and county, particularly in such areas as police and fire protection.

Another large advertisement was built around the theme "Suppose a smallpox epidemic hit Lexington." The basic message was that epidemics do not respect city-county boundaries any more than crime, traffic, or storm drainage problems do. Again, the point was to use the "crazy boundary" theme to help explain the tax-benefit argument.

The tax-benefit argument was also used in smaller ads, including a whole series placed in the classified columns. One classified ad read as follows: "Personal—Will the Lady Next Door Stop Complaining About Our Roads and Streets and Do Something About Them. We're Not Getting Any Sleep; Suggest You Try Voting For Merger on Election Day." Another classified, printed in white on a black background, read: "Tired of Paying Taxes For Services You Can't Receive? Vote Yes on Merger."

It was a major struggle to find a "catch-all" slogan that would summarize the cause. However, during the early stages of the campaign someone decided the promerger forces needed a bumper sticker. Steve Driesler did not rank the purchase of bumper stickers near the top of the list of priorities for the campaign. However, he did agree to order a relatively small number of bumper stickers bearing the slogan "We've Got the Urge to Merge."

These bumper stickers became something of an overnight sensation in Lexington. Not only did the CIGG have to have more stickers printed, but it seized upon the slogan for use in a series of newspaper advertisements featuring the pictures of various community leaders. Alongside each picture appeared the statement "I'm [so and so] and I have the Urge to Merge."

The biggest drawback to radio, television, and newspaper advertising was that, in the Lexington setting, there was no way to pitch specialized messages to particular segments of the electorate. All three media reached the entire Lexington-Fayette County market area and then some. This meant that not only was the CIGG paying to reach people who were not even eligible to vote in the merger referendum because they lived outside Fayette County, but it could not use the mass media to focus on specific concerns of blacks, of city versus county residents, or of other groups. Yet the August 1972 survey had revealed the necessity to couch some of the general dimensions of the tax-benefit and regime-government themes in rather group-specific terms.

This is where the computerized mailing system proved to be a handy tool. Mailing was a high priority item in the CIGG budget, and it was decided to use the computerized system to carry both general and specific types of appeals. Thus every household with a registered voter received a card stressing the advantages of "Neighborhood Representation."[4] Cards sent to black voters on this theme touched on more specific concerns of blacks and were signed by several key black leaders.

Voters who lived in the areas covered by the court decision on annexation received an additional mailing from the CIGG. They received a card giving the date when their area was subject to annexation and stressing that the real choice was annexation versus merger, and that annexation would mean an immediate 67 percent increase in their property tax rate while merger would not.

Whatever the outcome, the leaders of the CIGG had put together a campaign that was completely in tune with a statement made by Makielski in *City-County Consolidation.* In order to win, Makielski asserted, "those favoring merger have had to be willing to campaign actively for it, to know their voters, to keep the issues in front of the citizenry, and to fight long and hard for the vote."[5]

Everyone connected with the promerger campaign in Lexington expected that a major, well-organized opposition campaign would be unleashed, probably during the last two or three weeks before the election. Much to everyone's surprise, however, no significant organized opposition developed in Lexington.

Some dissident city employees, drawn mainly from the city fire department, formed a group called WHAM—"Why Have a Merger?" WHAM purchased two or three small ads in the local newspapers soliciting money to fight merger and posted mimeographed notices around city hall asking city employees to contribute money to help save their civil service and pension rights. Apparently these pleas for funds were largely ignored. At least WHAM never used any public campaign tactics that could have cost more than $200 to $300. WHAM did manage to have a pickup truck with a large sign asking voters to lose their "urge to merge" driven up and down Main Street and out to some of the larger shopping centers. And the group bought some small signs that were posted at voting places on election day asking voters to "save the pensions of policemen and firemen" by voting against merger. But that was all.

Once it became clear that WHAM was going to wage its campaign against merger around the question of civil service and pension rights of city employees, the leaders of the CIGG began to worry about other things. It was hard to believe that many voters other than local government employees could be persuaded to structure their attitudes toward merger around this particular question. Furthermore, the general impression of those who spent time around city hall was that WHAM was not even making much headway among city employees. Much of the credit for this failure could be attributed to Mayor Pettit and Judge Stephens who, along with the author, spent many hours meeting with both city and county employees to explain and answer questions about the civil service and pension provisions of the proposed charter.[6]

No other organized group came out publicly against merger. Even the Fayette County Farm Bureau, which was on the CIGG's list of potential opponents, decided by a vote of nine to four of its board of directors to support merger.[7] This was considered a major coup, since farm bureaus in other communities had generally opposed city-county consolidation.

Much of the credit for this victory must be given to Ecton, who met with the directors prior to their vote on a motion to support merger. He had some help in the form of a copy of a letter from one of the officers in the Davidson County (Tennessee) Farm Bureau to the head of the Jefferson County (Kentucky) Farm Bureau. In one key paragraph of this letter, a copy of which had been forwarded to the CIGG, it was noted that while the Davidson County Farm Bureau had opposed merger in Nashville in 1958 and again in 1962, after almost a decade of experience with merger in Nashville and Davidson County, most of the farm interests in that community were more than satisfied with what merger had done for them.[8]

Other than WHAM, the only public resistance to merger in the Lexington setting came from several individuals. One was William Jacobs, a local lawyer who had served in the city Law Department during the Underwood regime. His major argument was that merger violated the provisions of the state constitution requiring cities with more than 100,000 population to be reclassified as first-class cities, and that, given this requirement, first-class city status for Lexington was a preferable alternative to merger. Other than writing a guest editorial for the *Lexington Leader* on this theme and engaging a few promerger spokesmen in debates before several small gatherings, Jacobs did little to carry his message to the local electorate.

Former Lexington Mayor Fred Fugazzi did even less to publicize his antimerger views. It became clear early in the campaign that Fugazzi opposed merger. At least his decision to abstain on the vote of the Chamber of Commerce board to endorse the charter seemed to confirm what many had suspected all along. But he made no public move until three days before the election, when he published a very long letter to the editor. His letter was so long that it exceeded the limits imposed by the local newspaper for such items. Out of respect for a former mayor, however, it was published in its entirety, but on page 23 of the newspaper, next to the classified ads.[9] Pettit's brief rejoinder scoring Fugazzi's "eleventh hour" blast, on the other hand, appeared on page 1 of the election eve edition.

The leaders of the promerger campaign knew Fugazzi preferred massive annexation over merger, and this position, along with some very questionable arguments about the projected costs of merger, came through in his November 4 letter. What perplexed some of the promerger leaders was why he waited so long to come out publicly against merger. The only logical explanation seemed to be that there had been considerable speculation that Tom Underwood would eventually attempt to lead an organized effort to defeat merger, and Fugazzi, it was argued in some circles, did not want to risk being associated with Underwood.

The only other person who surfaced as an ardent opponent of merger was Charles Gulley. No one seemed to know very much about Gulley, except that his style and manner of presenting arguments were like what people had come to expect from Underwood. And his rhetoric was straight out of the Underwood era in local politics.

Gulley pitched his campaign against merger almost exclusively to the attentive public. He attended meetings featuring promerger speakers where he would use the question-and-answer session to make minispeeches against merger. He agreed to debate promerger spokesmen before groups that had tried for months to find someone to assume the task of arguing against merger.[10] And he pushed the local radio and television stations to give him equal time on their public service programs. He got one of the few Underwood appointees who had stayed on the charter commission following Underwood's defeat in 1971 to appear with him on a televised public service program just before the election.[11]

No one could fault Gulley for lack of dedication. He worked hard at fighting merger, and he seemed to genuinely believe in the things he said. But no one in the CIGG considered him much of a threat.

The author, for example, remembers well the debate he had with Gulley before a class on government and politics sponsored by the local IBM plant for its employees. One of Gulley's major concluding arguments during the debate was that, if merger passed, local government would be taken over by University of Kentucky students. His basis for making this assertion was that the district representation scheme set forth in the charter would allow university students to dominate the proposed Urban County Council.

At the time, it seemed rather curious that Gulley would try to use this particular point before a group of IBM employees taking a class in government and politics. Most of the students in this class, according to the information given to the author by Carl Penske who taught the course, were either college graduates or highly trained technical and middle-management employees who had come up through the ranks at IBM.

In any event, the author soon discovered that all he had to do in response to Gulley's allegations was to reiterate two points that various students in the class had made in their questions to Gulley. First, only two of the twelve proposed single-member districts contained any significant numbers of UK students, which at best could give them some control over only two of fifteen seats on the Urban County Council. Second, most of these students were not registered to vote in Fayette County, which reduced even further the possibility of their exercising any real impact on local electoral politics.[12]

Gulley's response was that, even if these things were true, he would move out of Fayette County if merger passed.

Whether Gulley was a front man for Tom Underwood, or whether he was even encouraged by Underwood, is not very important. Underwood himself never came out publicly against merger. Nor did he ever say or do anything to provide the smallest shred of evidence that he was behind any other person or group opposing merger. There are those in the promerger movement in

Lexington who still wonder why Underwood never showed his colors. Some felt that perhaps he waited too long to see how the antimerger cause would do, and that by the time he saw any real movement to counter the promerger drive it was too late to raise the kind of money and organization needed to mount a really effective campaign against merger. Others believe that he knew from the outset that the cards were stacked against his trying to make merger the basis for a political comeback. Both the 1971 Kraft poll and the resounding defeat handed to the Underwood team during the 1971 city elections, it was argued, made him very reluctant to take on the role of leading any antimerger campaign.

Whatever his reasons, Underwood's refusal to become a visible leader in a campaign against merger began to irk some of the supporters of merger who genuinely hoped that Underwood would come out publicly against merger. The feeling was that, given the resounding defeat suffered by Underwood and his cohorts in the 1971 city elections, many undecided voters could be brought into the promerger campaign if Underwood opposed the idea. It was also argued that his opposition would help considerably in the task of reinforcing the feelings and attitudes of those who, according to the August 1972 survey, were already prepared to support merger on election day.

The key point to keep in mind, however, is that the promerger forces never faced a well-organized, well-financed opposition campaign aimed at the mass electorate. There were no attempts on the part of WHAM, Jacobs, Fugazzi, or Gulley to wage a mass advertising campaign against merger in the local press, radio, or television media. No mass mailings were made by any of the opponents of merger to offset the activities along this line by the promerger forces. No widespread efforts were made by the opposition forces to organize workers in the various precincts.[13] And, except for the signs posted by WHAM at various polling places there was nothing to suggest that there was any opposition at all to the merger question by the time the election rolled around.

It is difficult to explain why the antimerger campaign in Lexington was so weak and ineffective in comparison to campaigns in other settings. Perhaps it was because well-meaning and intelligent opponents of the scheme, like former Mayor Fred Fugazzi, wished to avoid the risk that Tom Underwood would unleash a campaign against merger that could only prove embarrassing to them. Yet one could not discount the fact that the promerger forces had made it very difficult for an opponent of merger to get a solid handle on the issue. Not only had the charter commission provided a comprehensive plan for merging the city and county governments which was very much in tune with the political realities of the local community, but the promerger forces had gotten the jump on any potential opposition in organizing an all-out campaign for voter support. Furthermore, the promerger forces had apparently succeeded in making merger a kind of community-wide cause not unlike a United Fund drive. As one opponent of merger put it in his letter to the editor just before election day, "Supporting merger had become the 'In Thing' to do in Lexington."

It began to rain several hours before the polls opened at 6:00 A.M., November 7, 1972, and it rained all day. Like many other promerger workers, the author worried about the possible impact the rain would have on voter turnout, and how a low turnout might affect the outcome of the merger referendum.

It did not help very much to recall that Marando had found little correlation between voter turnout and the success or failure of other merger referenda.[14] His findings were abstractions about other merger settings. Nor did it do much good to review the findings of the August 1972 survey of Lexington voters which clearly suggested that even if the rain limited voter turnout to those who felt strongly about the issue, the promerger forces would probably still have the edge. Merger was not the only item on the ballot that day. This was a presidential election year, and there was also a hot United States Senate race in Kentucky between former Governor Louie Nunn and Walter Dee Huddleston. Who could predict what kinds of attitudes would be brought to bear on the merger question by the stalwart supporters of Nixon, McGovern, Nunn, or Huddleston in Fayette County?

By late that afternoon reports were coming into CIGG headquarters that, despite the rain, voter turnout was running ahead of most preelection speculations.[15] Still, there was no way of knowing how many voters were casting ballots on the merger question.

The polls closed at 6:00 P.M. To speed things up, the CIGG had people in every precinct calling in the results on the merger question as soon as the printouts were removed from the machines and read by the precinct officials before being carried down to the courthouse for certification. By shortly after 6:30 P.M. all precinct returns had been tabulated. Merger had passed by a better than two-to-one margin.

According to the official returns, a record-smashing 62,197 voters had turned out to vote on November 7, 1972.[16] Over 81 percent of those who went to the polls cast a ballot on the merger question. The vote was 35,372 to 15,308 in favor of adopting the merger charter. In percentage terms, 69.8 percent of all those who voted on the question favored adoption of the charter.

Further analysis of the official returns confirmed several other points that had been indicated in the returns phoned into CIGG headquarters on election night. For example, merger failed to attract a majority in only 6 of the 117 precincts in Lexington and Fayette County. Five of these were rural precincts that were totally unaffected by the annexation threat. Yet support for merger even in these rural precincts, which had been largely written off by the promerger forces, ran over 41 percent. The other losing precinct was Highlawn, which was in the area affected by the 1975 portion of the court order regarding annexation. The results from Highlawn were very close—165 "Yes" to 176 "No" votes.

There were, of course, precincts where merger carried by only a handful of votes. One of them was the essentially rural precinct known as Man o' War, where merger carried by only 9 votes. The remaining half-dozen marginally promerger precincts were quite similar to the marginally antimerger precinct of Highlawn. They tended to be essentially white, lower-middle-class county precincts that had been included in either the 1975 or 1980 annexation order handed down by the local circuit court.

Otherwise the pattern of support was quite consistent. Most of the middle- and upper-middle-class county precincts affected by the annexation order voted heavily for merger. All city precincts went solidly for merger, including those that were predominantly black. For all practical purposes, the promerger victory could be counted as a clean sweep.

Most merger proposals fail to win voter approval. Over 75 percent of all city-county consolidation attempts that reach the referendum stage are defeated at the polls. Because they are the exception, some observers have argued that merger victories can be explained only in terms of unique, idiosyncratic situational factors in those communities where merger has won voter approval. This explanation, however, always poses a problem for social scientists. To talk about unique and idiosyncratic causes flies in the face of scientific inquiry, which places a premium on developing explanations based on predictable patterns.

It is even more disturbing when social scientists discover that the arguments supporting a "unique event" explanation are based primarily, if not wholly, on selected case study materials. Not only do case studies have a way of focusing attention upon the unique features of a particular event, they tend to be stated in language that makes it difficult to draw meaningful cross-situational comparisons. As a result, much of the very real utility of case study materials is ignored or gets lost in the controversy over meaning and terminology.

Once some of the underbrush is cleared away, however, the literature concerning the "unique event" argument begins to take on some useful meaning. We are still left with the problem of specifying precisely what combinations of seemingly promerger situational factors need to be present to ensure a merger victory. But we are, it seems to me, in a much better position to examine particular merger victories, including the Lexington case, within a larger and more meaningful context.

There can be little doubt that the particular combination of situational assets available to the promerger forces in Lexington was unique. Taken together, these assets lend considerable weight to the argument of Mayor Pettit and others that the sweeping support given merger during the 1972 referendum was due to a unique combination of fortuitous circumstances. Where else, they argue, could one possibly hope to find so much political harmony over merger, so many advantages presented to the promerger forces by the massive annexation threat, or such an irrational city-county boundary that made it easy to illustrate the concept of waste and inefficiency?

Yet beneath all the rhetoric about sheer luck one is forced to admit that the Lexington setting was unique only in terms of the number and combination of favorable situational factors. Whether merger would have succeeded had any one or more of these situational factors been absent is open to speculation. To judge by the findings of the August 1972 survey, it might have been easier to get along without the first-class city issue than the annexation threat. But beyond this, it is impossible to weigh even in crude terms how much each of these seemingly promerger situational factors contributed to the merger victory in Lexington.

The important point is that the Lexington situation was very much in tune with the generalizations drawn from the literature concerning other communities where merger proposals have succeeded. Each of the favorable situational factors in the Lexington setting allowed one or more groups of voters to link merger in a positive way to some very basic concern that could not be satisfied under the status quo.

The annexation threat allowed the promerger forces to hammer away at the fact that most fringe voters could not realistically consider merger versus the status quo. After that, it became a matter of trying to inform those affected by the annexation order that only the merger option provided a written guarantee that their property tax rates would not increase until increased urban services were made available. Annexation, according to the tradition followed in Lexington and elsewhere in Kentucky, meant a substantial hike in property tax rates with no guarantee when city services would be installed.

The first-class city threat, while perhaps not so clear-cut, did at least allow promerger forces to stress the fact that city voters also faced a situation in which the status quo was not a realistic option.

More important, it allowed the promerger forces to point out to city voters, and especially black city voters, that only by choosing the merger option could they hope to get district representation.

Third, the "crazy boundary" between the city and county, which would probably stand out as a very unusual feature in the Lexington setting, proved a useful asset for the promerger forces. Not only did it provide a dramatic visual illustration of the absurdities of trying to maintain two governments, it provided example after example of how local jurisdictional lines can get in the way of providing such things as adequate police and fire protection to both city and county residents. Furthermore, it cut across the "mosaic of social worlds" in such a haphazard way that one would have been hard pressed to convince very many voters that the boundary helped protect and preserve their socioeconomic or life-style interests.

Several other situational factors have been touted by some local observers as major contributors to the success of the Lexington merger effort. For example, considerable credit has been given to the fact that there was only one incorporated municipality within the boundaries of Fayette County. As indicated earlier in this study, however, the Lexington setting was not particularly unusual in terms of its governmental fragmentation score. Furthermore, it should be recalled that the won-lost record in those communities with only two existing units of government was not much different from that found for all merger referendum situations. In short, Lexington happened to be a good setting for *considering* merger because it had only two units of government. But it still stands out as one of the relatively few communities with similar fragmentation scores that managed a merger victory.

Much the same can be said about the argument that the promerger forces benefited from not having to secure separate majorities in the city and county. The fact is that merger would have carried in Lexington even if the law had required separate majorities among city and noncity voters.

Another explanation for the success of the merger effort in Lexington has been that blacks constituted only a very small proportion of the local electorate. There is no doubt that Lexington blacks were numerically a long way from being able to consider "taking over" either unit of local government. But again, there have been relatively few merger settings where blacks have been in such a position. And among those instances where merger has passed, the general situation has been one in which blacks could hope to improve their representation in local government under merger or face the prospects of continued dilution of their voting strength under existing at-large systems of representation through annexation. Certainly the Lexington setting was not atypical in this respect.

All in all, a very strong case can be made for the argument that the Lexington setting differed from most of the other "merger winners" described in the literature only in degree. The uniqueness of the Lexington setting can be found only in the fact that it happened to contain an unusually large number of situational factors that could be exploited by the promerger forces. Taken individually or collectively, the fundamental importance of these situational assets in the Lexington setting is that they provided a means for a wide variety of voters to link merger with some rather specific goal that could not be achieved under the status quo. And this, of course, is the underlying premise of the generalization drawn earlier from the literature concerning other "unique event" merger victories.

10

Launching the New Government

ALTHOUGH THE voters had approved the adoption of the Lexington charter in November of 1972, it could not be put into effect until January 1, 1974. The Peak-McCann bill (KRS 67A) stated, in effect, that no comprehensive plan of urban county government adopted by referendum could become effective until the term of the county judge for the county in question had expired. In the Lexington case, this meant waiting until the term of incumbent Fayette County Judge Robert Stephens expired on December 31, 1973.

There were those who were not entirely happy about this delay. However, thirteen months proved to be a very short time to work out the many complex details for implementing the new system. Furthermore, both the local circuit court and the state Court of Appeals had made it clear in their earlier decisions upholding the constitutionality of the enabling legislation that the validity of KRS 67A did not extend to any charter or comprehensive plan of urban county government adopted under its provisions.[1] Thus, the proponents of the Lexington charter faced the additional problem of trying to secure a definitive court ruling on the constitutionality of the charter during this same thirteen-month period.

Roy Holsclaw and Ronald Pinchback, both of whom had supported merger, led the fight on the legal front by filing a class-action suit challenging the constitutionality of every article and section of the Lexington charter shortly after the referendum.[2] Several companion suits were filed later by groups interested in clarifying the legal status of specific provisions of the adopted charter.[3] Another companion suit was filed by William Jacobs, a local lawyer who had opposed merger on the grounds that it violated the state constitutional requirement that every city with more than 100,000 people be classified as a first-class city.

Although the adopted charter contained contingency provisions for delaying its implementation beyond the January 1, 1974, deadline, every effort was made to persuade the court of the urgency of the situation. The court, in turn, responded by giving the case very prompt attention. Thus, despite the number and complexity of legal questions that had been raised, the local circuit court managed to render a decision in the case of *Holsclaw et al.* v. *Stephens et al.* by September 17, 1973.

In that decision, Fayette Circuit Court Judge George Barker upheld the constitutionality of the charter in almost every respect. Several sections of the charter were ruled invalid and several other contested provisions were declared unjusticiable at that time.[4] But none of these exceptions struck at the heart of the charter.

Unfortunately, only three and one-half months remained before the new charter was scheduled to be put into effect. Even with a concerted effort by all parties to the suit, it would be difficult to obtain a definitive opinion from the state Court of Appeals before January 1, 1974. In fact, there were some discussions among various merger supporters about whether to proceed with the implementation of the charter with only the circuit court's favorable decision to go on. "What would happen," some people asked, "if the charter was put into effect and the Court of Appeals declared it unconstitutional, or so emasculated it that the new government could not function?"

Much of this kind of talk was put to rest when the Court of Appeals agreed on November 2, 1973, to consolidate all of the cases on appeal involving the charter and to advance the case on its docket. December 10 was declared as the deadline for filing all briefs, and several members of the court were quoted as saying it was very important that a decision be handed down before the charter was implemented.[5]

The court met the January 1 deadline, but with little time to spare. Its six to one decision upholding the basic provisions of the Lexington charter was announced on Friday, December 28, 1973.[6]

The lone dissenter was Justice Earl T. Osborne, who had been quoted earlier as saying to the attorneys present when the deadline for briefs was established: "You fellows can file your briefs; all I need is a copy of the Constitution and the charter."[7]

Space will not permit a thorough and detailed review of the forty-page decision handed down by the Kentucky Court of Appeals. It is sufficient to note here that several provisions of the charter that Judge Barker had struck down, including the one that allowed the mayor to succeed himself, were restored by the Court of Appeals. Most of these restored items had been declared invalid by Judge Barker because of his ruling that an urban county government was, in the final analysis, a municipality and therefore subject to the provisions of the state constitution dealing with cities.

The Court of Appeals explained at considerable length the reasoning behind its view that the Lexington charter had created a new and unique form or classification of local government. It was "neither a city government nor a county government," the court declared. It was an "entirely new creature in which are combined all the powers of a county government and all of the powers possessed by that class of cities to which the largest city in the county belongs."[8]

This allowed the court not only to restore some of the provisions that Judge Barker had struck down, but also to abandon the very tricky and potentially far-reaching conclusions drawn by Barker when it came to deciding whether the district representation provisions of the charter were valid. By adopting the "unique form" argument, the Court of Appeals found no reason to pit section 160 of the state constitution against the state bill of rights.[9] It could simply declare that as a unique but valid classification of local government, an urban county could elect some or all of its council members from single-member districts simply because there were no prohibitions against such a system in the constitution.

None of the relatively minor details that the court refused to uphold posed any serious problems. The new government could survive such things as being forced to pay the members of the county Fiscal Court.[10] Nor was it too difficult to accept the ruling that the charter could not disband the local urban renewal authority and place its functions under a line department, for the court had sustained every other effort to get rid of independent boards, commissions, and authorities.

Throughout the months of litigation over the constitutionality of the Lexington charter, action was being taken on another very crucial front. Proceeding on the assumption that the courts would eventually uphold the validity of the charter, Fayette County Judge Robert Stephens and Lexington Mayor Foster Pettit appointed a small task force shortly after the November 1972 merger referendum was over. This task force was to study the administrative problems associated with implementing the new charter and develop plans and recommendations for making the transition between the old and new systems of government.

The task force was headed by Thomas Sullivan, a management specialist at the local IBM plant, who was given a leave by his employer to work full-time on the project. He was assisted by several key administrators from the city and county governments, and by the author, who served as a part-time consultant representing the charter commission.

Much of the work done by the task force focused on researching and developing alternative ways of handling such important but sensitive matters as merging city and county salary and benefit schedules, reorganizing various administrative agencies, and outlining a series of temporary job titles. In addition, it spent considerable time developing recommendations for combining the existing city and county budgetary, accounting, and personnel systems to fit at least the initial requirements of the charter.

Few observers of the Lexington merger process, including those who were deeply involved in drafting the charter, seemed to appreciate the complexity and importance of these seemingly routine administrative tasks. Yet many of these questions continued to plague the mayor and council of the new merged government throughout most of its first three years of operation. One can only speculate about how much more difficult the task would have been without the cooperation of the former city and county governments in establishing a task force to research and develop some guidelines for addressing these problems.

Perhaps the greatest contribution of the task force was a series of contractual agreements to merge the city and county police, fire, and parks departments prior to the formal implementation of the Lexington charter. The idea of merging the city and county police departments under the provisions of an existing state statute on intergovernmental cooperation had been discussed on several occasions before the adoption of the merger charter in Lexington. These discussions, however, inevitably became bogged down over the provision in the state law which seemed to limit such contracts to the terms of those officials who made them. This provision raised a host of questions about what would happen if such a contractual merger were to be voided by some future mayor or county judge.[11]

Once the Lexington merger charter was adopted, however, the specter of a contract being terminated by some future city or county administration became less frightening. Thus, the task force was able to convince the city and county police departments that they had little to lose in the summer of 1973 by signing a contract to merge police operations pending the actual implementation of the adopted charter. Shortly after the police contract was adopted, a similar arrangement was completed with the city and county fire departments. And by the fall of 1973, the task force had worked out a contract merging the city and county parks departments.

A number of bargains had to be struck to put these contract mergers into operation. The city police chief became the head of the newly merged police department, while the ex-county police chief agreed to be an assistant chief. The city fire chief took over the reigns of the merged fire department with the consent of the chief of the smaller county fire department. And the head of the city parks department agreed to allow his county counterpart to take charge of the newly formed city-county park operations. Variations in age and personal career interests made these bargains possible. The task force was thus able to put the concept of merger into operation in three very critical functional areas several months before the local governments would have to implement a totally new system of government and administration.

Despite these accomplishments, it was clearly understood by everyone associated with the work of the task force that article 15 of the Lexington charter designated the first mayor and the members of the first Urban County Council as the *official* body for working out the details for launching the new government. Technically there was no way that the charter commission could have required the existing city and county governments to do anything toward paving the way for implementing the charter. The best that could be done was to charge the first mayor and council with certain responsibilities during the brief interim between their election and the proposed effective date of the charter.[12]

Unfortunately, there was no way under Kentucky law to elect the first mayor and the members of the first council until the next regularly scheduled general election following the adoption of the Lexington charter. This meant waiting until November 6, 1973, before any official action could be taken to work out many of the details surrounding the implementation of the charter. Thus, the official lead time for implementing the charter had been cut from thirteen months to less than two months. As it happened, even this short period was not available in Lexington.

At the outset of the 1973 urban county mayor and council races, most observers seemed confident that Lexington Mayor Foster Pettit would be the first mayor of the new government. County Judge Robert Stephens had decided not to run for the post, leaving Pettit to face only one challenger—Municipal Court Judge James Amato. Amato was not a particularly well-known political leader in the community at the time. Nor had he been involved with the seemingly popular merger effort, whereas Pettit had been out in front of the promerger campaign all the way.

As the November 6, 1973, general election drew near, however, it became more and more apparent that the Pettit-Amato race would be very close. Backed by a number of leading Fayette County Democrats who apparently felt that Pettit had taken his role as a nonpartisan mayor of the city too seriously, Amato unleashed a well-organized and well-financed attack upon Pettit's tax policies and his alleged lack of concern over Lexington's traffic problems. Meanwhile, the Pettit campaign was based on the calm assumption that Pettit's 1971 victory over Underwood and his open support for merger in 1972 would carry him over any opposition.

When the returns for the November 6, 1973, election were recorded, they showed that Amato had won by a slim 112-vote margin. However, the Pettit forces took the case to court on the grounds that the name strips for the two rows of levers that had been set aside for urban county mayor and council candidates had apparently been reversed on the voting machine used in the Aylesford precinct. This meant, according to Pettit, that every vote cast for him in that precinct was recorded on the official printout on the back of the machine as a vote for Amato, and vice versa.

Although none of the council races were affected by this apparent foul-up, the outcome of the Amato-Pettit contest depended on how the court decided to resolve the situation. If the court decided to ignore the question raised by Pettit, then Amato would win by 112 votes. If it decided to throw out the returns from the Aylesford precinct, Amato would have remained the victor, but by only a 29-vote margin. But if the results recorded on the machine printout for the Aylesford precinct were simply reversed to match the order of things on the front of the machine, Pettit would win by 54 votes.[13]

Because of the urgency of the question, the local court did its utmost to render a decision before the new charter was scheduled to go into effect. It announced on December 27, 1973, that the "official" returns from the Aylesford precinct for the mayoral race were to be reversed and that Pettit was to be declared the winner by a margin of 54 votes.[14]

As expected, Amato immediately filed an appeal with the Kentucky Court of Appeals. Although the appeals court was expected to give the case a very high priority, no one expected a decision on the matter by the time the new charter was scheduled to go into effect.

As it turned out, the fifteen members of the first Urban County Council were sworn into office at a brief ceremony held at Transylvania University on the morning of January 1, 1974. Foster Pettit presided at the occasion, but was not sworn in as mayor. James Amato stood in the back of the auditorium with several of his friends and political supporters.[15] The charter was in effect. The new council had been officially sworn in. But the new Lexington-

Fayette Urban County Government was technically without a mayor.

Finally, on January 15, 1974, the Kentucky Court of Appeals handed down its decision upholding the local circuit court.[16] The votes cast for mayor in the Aylesford precinct were to be reversed, giving Pettit the victory, and two days later, H. Foster Pettit was sworn in as the first mayor of the Lexington-Fayette Urban County Government at a regularly scheduled Thursday night meeting of the council.[17]

Although Amato never challenged Pettit's decision to preside over council meetings during the period between the disputed election and the handing down of the Court of Appeals decision in the matter, the council found it rather difficult to deal with the concept of an "acting mayor." Some of the indecision displayed by the council during this period could also be attributed to the fact that this larger and more diversified legislative body was composed mainly of political neophytes who had never met a public payroll.[18] In addition, a number of rather critical decisions simply could not be confronted by the council until the question of who would be the mayor had been resolved.

For example, the council could not address such matters as the budget for the new government until it was decided who would have the legal authority to exercise the budgetary powers assigned to the mayor by the charter.[19] Nor was there any way for the council to begin the task of filling key administrative positions called for by the charter until it was known whether Pettit or Amato would end up with the power to nominate individuals to be approved or disapproved by the council to serve in these positions.

In short, the bizarre events surrounding the election of the first mayor of the Lexington-Fayette Urban County Government seriously undercut the provisions of the charter pertaining to the transitional role of the new mayor and council during the period between their election and the effective date of the charter. And they continued to plague the performance of the new government throughout the first two weeks of its official existence.

It was not the most auspicious beginning for the new system of local government. Yet the council handled the situation with considerable patience and restraint. The council may have been reluctant, and in some cases unable, to move ahead with implementing many of the provisions of the new charter. But none of its members overtly risked alienating either contender for the office of mayor by becoming publicly embroiled in the legal controversy between Pettit and Amato. It was almost as if the members of the new council had deliberately decided to do what they could toward organizing themselves into an effective legislative body while they waited for the courts to tell them who the first mayor of the new government would be.

The important point, however, is that the charter for the Lexington-Fayette Urban County Government was put into effect on the prescribed date virtually as it had been written by the local merger commission. It had survived an exhaustive test of the constitutionality of its various provisions before both the local circuit court and the state Court of Appeals without suffering major damage. And it rested on a legal foundation that recognized all basic and fundamental assumptions made by the local charter commission that drew it up. Furthermore, it should be recalled that by January 1, 1974, several sizable and important functions of local government were already operating as merged departments under contractual arrangements between the old city and county governments.

It is beyond the scope of this study to examine the performance of the Lexington-Fayette Urban County Government since it was implemented on January 1, 1974. Indeed, it may be too soon even to attempt such a task. Nevertheless, several observations seem to be in order as Lexington prepares to embark upon its fifth year under merged government.

First, the Lexington experience suggests that it requires between two and three years to complete many of the complex changes called for in a typical merger charter. For example, it took almost two years to recruit and hire a chief administrative officer, department commissioners, and several key division directors. This was not the result of any scheme to thwart the will of those who voted for merger. It simply required considerable time and energy to fill top level administrative positions while coping with the day-to-day problems generated by the necessity of reorganizing agencies and procedures.

In the area of budgeting, the charter called for the adoption of a five-year capital improvements program along with the first full fiscal year operating budget starting on July 1, 1974. The capital improvements program was to be updated at the start of each successive fiscal year. Unfortunately, this requirement of the charter has not yet been met. Although the 1976–1977 five-year capital improvements program came closer to hitting the mark, both the mayor and the CAO have admitted that it falls short of the kind of document envisioned by the charter.

One reason for the difficulty here has been that long-range capital improvement programming was a totally new idea in Lexington. Neither the former city nor the county had ever engaged in the type of capital improvement programming called for by the new charter. Furthermore, the delays in hiring administrative personnel to perform the tasks involved in creating such a program, along with the burdens associated with coping with the many day-to-day problems of operating a new system of government, continually plagued those who were concerned about this particular feature of the charter.

In a similar vein, the charter called upon the new government to develop a totally new and comprehensive classified civil service system within two years. In fact, the final details for such a plan, including a complete reclassification of all civil service positions and a new salary schedule tied to the reclassification, were presented to the council in February 1977. Again, some of the delay in implementing this provision of the charter can be attributed to the problem of hiring qualified personnel to perform the task. Some of it can be attributed to the fact that merger created many more immediate and critical administrative problems, especially during the first year or two of operation, than had been anticipated. Much of it, however, must be assigned to the sheer magnitude and complexity of tasks specified by the charter.

There are those, including some members of the Urban County Council, who blamed these delays on the mayor and on those who had been hired to administer the new government. As a member of the council since January 1, 1976, I can appreciate the legitimacy of this line of argument in some cases. Occasionally the council, out of sheer frustration, has had to remind the administration to push ahead on various projects associated with implementing the charter. There have even been occasions when the council has felt obliged to assume considerable control over administrative problems, such as preparing for the implementation of a major governmental space study ordered by the new mayor and council shortly after the charter went into effect.

On balance, however, it should be noted that the problems associated with implementing the Lexington merger charter proved far more complex and time-consuming than most members of the council or the charter commission had anticipated. Furthermore, it must be remembered that all of the budgetary, administrative, and personnel changes required by the charter had to be made while the new government struggled to maintain all of the various day-to-day services of local government.

Having said this, it seems appropriate to make a second basic observation about the experience with merger in Lexington. The shift from a purely at-large to a predominantly single-member district system of representation produced a major change in the local decision-making process. Not only did district representation introduce a more varied and overtly segmented set of interests into council deliberations, it tended to heighten and expose conflicts over various public policy questions. This, in turn, has tended to produce delays and equivocation in making decisions.

Since most other successful merger proposals have also called for an emphasis upon district representation, it is important to point out that the shift to such system tends to generate ambivalence among citizens. As a district representative on the Lexington-Fayette Urban County Council, I have found many citizens very supportive of having what they consider to be their own voice on the council when it comes to deciding such things as proposed zoning changes in their neighborhood, getting their street on the schedule for resurfacing, or obtaining special consideration from the division of police to enforce traffic laws in their particular neighborhood. On the other hand, many of these same citizens are equally quick to condemn the mayor and council for spending too much time arguing over what they consider to be simple, straightforward questions. In short, the Lexington experience suggests that, while many people seem to prefer the idea of having district representation, they are not always willing to pay the price in terms of heightened conflict and delay in the decision-making process.

In addition to all of the administrative and organizational problems posed by the new charter, the mayor and council of the new government had to contend with at least one other serious problem during its first three years of operation. The mere existence of a new system of local government seemed to generate a whole new set of conflicting demands and expectations among various individuals and groups in the community. Elected officials found themselves confronted with scores of requests from both government administrators and private citizens to create or expand public services and programs thought to be in keeping with the "reform spirit" of the merger charter. Others pleaded for cuts in the budgets of various agencies to insure that the economies and efficiencies promised by merger could be made.

Perhaps the most troublesome problem along these lines grew out of the provisions of the charter concerning the expansion of such urban services as sanitary sewers, street lights, and garbage collection. Despite the efforts of the charter commission and the promerger campaign organization to explain the concept of taxing and services districts, many citizens continued to believe that urban services would be extended to former county areas immediately after merger went into effect. Others displayed genuine shock when they were told that these services would not be extended free of charge.

Sanitary sewers became the biggest headache, primarily because the first mayor and council decided to concentrate their efforts on extending this service to those areas where malfunctioning septic tanks had created major health problems. Unfortunately, many of the areas most in need of sewers happened to include many homeowners living on modest and/or fixed incomes. Furthermore, the government tried to embark on a major expansion of sanitary sewers before it had fully explored all of the existing state laws for financing such projects, and before it had secured the kind of technical and administrative capability to handle such a complex undertaking.

Trouble erupted almost immediately after the government announced plans to begin work on several major sewer projects. After a series of stormy public hearings in 1974 and 1975, the mayor and council decided to call a halt on the sewer projects until a better package could be developed.

Given the difficulties encountered by the new government, it came as no surprise that Charles Gulley and several others who had opposed merger during the 1972 referendum campaign decided to sponsor a petition to get rid of merger. Technically, the demerger petition sought to have an amendment to the charter placed on the ballot calling for the abolition of the merger government and a return to the old system of separate city and county governments.[20]

The petition drive began several months after the new charter was put into effect. Although Gulley and his associates failed to secure enough signatures to have the proposed demerger amendment placed on the November 1974 ballot, they continued their efforts.[21] By the August 6 deadline for having the question placed on the November 1975 ballot, they had filed more than 9,500 signatures with the county clerk. Assuming that all names on the petition represented registered voters in Fayette County, this seemed to be a truly impressive display of support for demerger.

Up to this point, few promerger supporters seemed willing to take Gulley and his small band of antimerger activists very seriously. Some had felt that there was little chance that they would ever get enough signatures to get the question on the ballot. Others argued that even if they did get on the ballot, the demerger amendment would be defeated. The question was repeatedly asked: "Who could possibly be in favor of such an absurd idea?" It sounded almost like an echo from the debate over whether the promerger forces ought to mount an all-out campaign back in 1972.

Since only 6,102 signatures were needed to place the demerger amendment on the ballot, there seemed to be little hope that a careful review of the signatures on the petition would be of much use.

Nevertheless, the mayor requested that the county clerk check the validity of every name on the petition. The task required several weeks of concerted effort. But shortly after the count began, reports began to circulate that many invalid signatures were being found. By the end of August, the list of valid signatures of registered voters had shrunk to only 99 names more than the 6,102 needed.[22] And by the time the list had been culled for duplicate signatures, the demerger petition was 420 signatures short of the required number.[23] Over 4,000 signatures had been thrown out, because they were unreadable, not those of registered voters, or duplicates of valid signatures.

No systematic study has been made to date of the individuals who signed the demerger petition. Thus, it is impossible to say whether the list was composed primarily of those who had opposed merger from the start, or whether it was made up largely of former merger supporters who had been converted to the cause led by known antimerger people. Nor were any scientific polls or surveys conducted to indicate whether or not the demerger forces would have had a reasonable chance of winning voter approval if their proposal had been placed on the 1975 ballot.

A careful examination of the addresses of the signers, however, revealed several interesting facts. First, over 55 percent of all signatures on the petition were obtained from persons living in the proposed sanitary sewer project areas. (Less than 23 percent of all adults in Fayette County lived in these proposed sewer areas.) The next most discernible group of demerger petitioners came from either rural areas or those fringe areas where merger had attracted the least amount of voter support in 1972.

In addition to the turmoil and controversy created by the 1974–1975 sewer expansion effort, one could mention several other factors that could conceivably have led to the kind of citizen unrest that Gulley and his friends tried to exploit. For example, in 1975 the results of state-ordered reassessment of all nonfarm property in Fayette County were announced. Many homeowners were quite upset when they discovered that the assessed valuation of property they had owned for eight to ten years had more than doubled. Nor did one have to seek out inattentive and ill-informed citizens to discover that the new urban county government, rather than the state, was receiving the lion's share of the blame.

Hard feelings left over from the very close and controversial mayor's race in 1973 and a heated fireman's strike over collective bargaining in 1974 provided additional reasons for various citizens to lash out at the new government by signing the demerger petition. Yet despite over a year and a half of effort the demerger project failed. And an effort to launch another drive to get the question placed on the November 1976 ballot never got beyond the stage of circulating printed notices that a new petition was available.

Regardless of how one interprets the events surrounding the first three years of experience with merger in Lexington, including the trauma associated with the unsuccessful demerger effort, several very positive points need to be made before this study is concluded.

First, one of the most immediate and obvious benefits of merger was the elimination of jurisdictional conflicts between city and county police and fire units caused by that crazy city-county boundary. In the area of fire protection, this fact alone resulted in a substantial reduction of fire insurance rates for property owners throughout the built-up area that had been outside the old city limits. And it led to a slight reduction in fire insurance premiums for many rural dwellers. It seems reasonable to argue that if there were a nationally recognized set of standards for evaluating the performance of police departments similar to those employed by the fire insurance industry to set fire insurance rates, the results of merger in the area of police protection would have been equally impressive.

Second, the council has recently adopted a complicated set of proposals that will virtually eliminate most of the illogical and often expensive effects of the former boundary upon the delivery of such services as street lights, sanitary sewers, and garbage collection. This was a major undertaking, but it can now be said that all those who had city sewers available prior to merger are now either paying for them or are obliged to begin paying for them. And major strides have been made to rationalize the areas served by public refuse and garbage collection services.

Finally, after backing down on the expansion of sanitary sewers in 1975, the Lexington-Fayette Urban County Government is now in a position to proceed with this much needed program. In 1976 the local government got state legislation passed to allow a more flexible and equitable method of assessing property owners for the cost of installing sewer lines. In addition it adopted a financial assistance plan to help the needy to pay their fair share of the cost. And it has created the kind of technical and administrative machinery needed to design and execute sewer projects.

In short, after four years of operation, the Lexington-Fayette Urban County Government is on the verge of fulfilling many of the promises made by the proponents of merger. And despite inflation, and the tremendous start-up cost of a totally new system of government, it has managed to do all of this without raising tax rates. True, the state-mandated reassessment in 1975 increased the revenues of the new government. But the council was able to help offset the impact of this event upon property owners by granting a slight tax rate reduction.

Beyond this, it is difficult to measure the impact of merger. Part of the difficulty is that there are a variety of reasons why various people initiated, promoted, and eventually voted for the idea. By the same token, there are a wide variety of reasons, some logical and some not so logical, for people either to praise or to condemn the performance of a merged government. In the final analysis, one must return to perhaps the only valid reason for attempting city-county consolidation—namely, that it provides a vehicle for trying to cope rationally with the many problems confronting communities like Lexington.

Notes

CHAPTER 1

1. The term "urban county government" is unique in the annals of city-county consolidation. It was imposed on the residents of Lexington-Fayette County, Kentucky, by the enabling legislation passed by the Kentucky General Assembly in 1970 and was directly related to the provision in the Kentucky State Constitution forbidding the abolition of counties. From a constitutional perspective, it made sense for the enabling statute to retain the word *county* in the references to the new system that might evolve under its provision. See KRS 67A.040–090.

2. See, for example: David Booth, *Metropolitics: The Nashville Consolidation* (East Lansing: Michigan State University, 1963), pp. 37–56; Schley R. Lyons, *Citizen Attitudes and Metropolitan Government: City-County Consolidation in Charlotte* (Charlotte: University of North Carolina at Charlotte, 1972), pp. 24–72; and W. E. Lyons and Richard L. Engstrom, "Socio-Political Crosspressures and Attitudes toward Political Integration of Urban Governments," *Journal of Politics* 35 (August 1973): 682–711.

CHAPTER 2

1. Joseph Zimmerman, "Metropolitan Reform in the U.S.: An Overview," *Public Administration Review* 30 (September-October 1970): 531–33.

2. David Lawrence and H. Rutherford Turnbull III, "UNIGOV: City-County Consolidation in Indianapolis," *Popular Government* 36 (November 1969): 18–20; and Andrew Gruse, "Las Vegas-Clark County Consolidation: A Unique Event in Search of a Theory," *Nevada Public Affairs Report* 14 (March 1976): 1–9.

3. For a discussion of the arguments and assumptions of the earlier civic references see Paul Studenski, *The Government of Metropolitan Areas* (New York: National Municipal League, 1930), pp. 7–42, 388–90.

4. For an excellent analysis of contemporary civic reformer ideas and assumptions see H. Paul Freisema, "The Metropolis and the Maze of Local Government," *Urban Affairs Quarterly* 2 (December 1972): 68–90.

5. This definition has been adopted by the National Association of Counties, which has recently assumed the task of compiling information about consolidation efforts throughout the United States. See *County News*, December 15, 1972, p. 6.

6. Donald Rowat, *Your Local Government* (Toronto: Macmillan, 1962), p. 24. See also *Report of the Royal Commission on Metropolitan Toronto* (Toronto: Province of Ontario, June 1965), pp. 26–29; and *Report of the Niagara Region Local Government Review* (Toronto: Province of Ontario, August 1966), pp. 59–67.

7. S. J. Makielski, Jr., *City-County Consolidation: A Guide for Virginians* (Charlottesville: University of Virginia, 1971), p. 17.

8. Schley Lyons, *Citizen Attitudes and Metropolitan Government* (Charlotte: University of North Carolina at Charlotte, 1972), pp. 1–5.

9. David Booth, *Metropolitics: The Nashville Consolidation* (East Lansing: Michigan State University, 1963), p. 84.

10. Ibid., p. 85.

11. For an excellent summation of this argument see Friesema, "Metropolis and Maze."

12. Oliver Williams et al., *Suburban Differences and Metropolitan Policies* (Philadelphia: University of Pennsylvania Press, 1965), pp. 17–74, 289–312. See also: Friesema, "Metropolis and Maze," pp. 78–80; and Scott Greer, *Governing the Metropolis* (New York: John Wiley and Sons, 1962), pp. 23–58.

13. Williams et al., *Suburban Differences,* pp. 28–29.

14. Friesema, "Metropolis and Maze," pp. 68–73.

15. Brett Hawkins, "Life-Style, Demographic Distance, and Voter Support of City-County Consolidation," (*Southwestern*) *Social Science Quarterly* 48 (December 1967): 333.

16. Walter C. Kaufman and Scott Greer, "Voting in a Metropolitan Community: An Application of Social Area Analysis," *Social Forces* 38 (March 1960): 196–204; and Basil Zimmer and Amos Hawley, "Resistance to Unification in a Metropolitan Community," in Morris Janowitz, ed., *Community Political Systems* (New York: Free Press, 1961), pp. 146–84.

17. Brett Hawkins, "Fringe-City Life-Style Distance and Fringe Support of Political Integration," *American Journal of Sociology* 74 (November 1968): 248–55.

18. Makielski, *City-County Consolidation,* p. 18.

19. At least an analysis by the author of the voting returns by precinct on a consolidation proposal in Augusta-Richmond County, Georgia, indicated that in the city of Augusta, where the population was about 51 percent black, the vote was overwhelmingly proconsolidation in all white precincts and overwhelmingly anticonsolidation in all black precincts.

20. This is clearly suggested by Lee Sloan and Robert French, "Black Rule in the Urban South?" *Trans-Action* 19 (November-December 1971): 30–31.

21. Richard Engstrom and W. E. Lyons, "Black Control or Consolidadation: The Fringe Response," *Social Science Quarterly* 53 (June 1972): 161–67.

22. Thomas Scott, "Metropolitan Governmental Reorganization Proposals," *Western Political Quarterly* 21 (June 1968): 501–2.

23. Booth, *Metropolitics,* pp. 86–87.

24. Vincent Marando, "Factors Affecting Voter Response to City-County Consolidation" (Paper delivered before the Conference on Integration of Metropolitan Government, Louisiana State University at New Orleans, 1972). See also Marando, "Political and Social Variables in City-County Consolidation Referenda," *Polity* 4 (Summer 1972): 512–22.

25. W. E. Lyons and Richard Engstrom, "Socio-Political Crosspressures and Attitudes toward Political Integration of Urban Governments," *Journal of Politics* 35 (August 1973): 682–711.

CHAPTER 3

1. For an excellent discussion of how complications in the spatial contours of social worlds tend to work in favor of maintaining political fragmentation in metropolitan areas see Oliver Williams et al., *Suburban Differences and Metropolitan Policies* (Philadelphia: University of Pennsylvania Press, 1965), pp. 28–30.

2. For a detailed description of the physical, social, and economic characteristics of Lexington see *A Growing Community* (Lexington, Ky.: Lexington-Fayette County Planning Commission, 1973), pp. 2–159.

3. Lee Sloan and Robert French, "Black Rule in the Urban South?" *Trans-Action* 19 (November-December 1971): 30.

4. The Augusta-Richmond County, Georgia, setting, with a central city slightly more than 50 percent black and a fringe area over 76 percent white, provides the best fit. Other communities that come reasonably close in terms of city-fringe black populations include: Richmond-Henrico County, Virginia (42 and 5 percent black); Macon-Bibb County, Georgia (44 and 22); Brunswick-Glynn County, Georgia (41 and 13); Jacksonville-Duvall County, Florida (41 and 9); and Nashville-Davidson County, Tennessee (37 and 5).

5. Sloan and French, "Black Rule," p. 32. The voting behavior of Nashville blacks in 1958 is confirmed by David Booth, *Metropolitics* (East Lansing: Michigan State University, 1963), pp. 34–35.

6. Sloan and French, "Black Rule," p. 32.

7. Schley Lyons, *Citizen Attitudes and Metropolitan Government* (Charlotte: University of North Carolina at Charlotte, 1972), p. 30.

8. Ibid., pp. 30–31.

9. Ibid., p. 53.

10. Booth, *Metropolitics,* p. 73.

11. Ibid., p. 88.

12. Ibid., p. 87.

13. According to state law (KRS 81.140), the only remedy available for those protesting a proposed annexation ordinance is to remonstrate in court. If more than 50 percent of the property owners in an area scheduled to be annexed petition the court for relief, the burden of proof is placed on the city. Under such circumstances the city must prove that not being allowed to carry out the annexation ordinance will do it irreparable harm. If less than 50 percent of the affected property owners remonstrate, the burden of proof is placed on the petitioners.

14. Officially the report was entitled: "Annexation Plan for the City of Lexington and Fayette County," submitted by the Spindletop Research Corporation of Lexington. It was usually referred to as the Spindletop Report.

15. There was some speculation, for example, that the Underwood forces were concerned about the fact that many of the areas to be annexed were socially and economically similar to the kinds of precincts in the city where they had performed most poorly during the 1968 election.

16. The proposed merged government charter called for the new mayor and council to be elected in November 1973 and take office January 1, 1974.

17. Based on 1972 figures, the increase would have been approximately 69 percent.

18. Section 172A of the state constitution, as adopted by the voters in 1969, said in part: "The General Assembly may provide for reasonable differences in the rate of ad valorem taxation within different areas of the same taxing districts on that class of property which includes the surface of the land. Those differences shall relate directly to differences between non-revenue-producing governmental services and benefits giving land urban character which are furnished in one or several areas in contrast to other areas of the taxing district."

19. Section 156, *Constitution of the Commonwealth of Kentucky.*

20. The point was made by Mr. Thomas Underwood at a hearing of the Sub-Committee on Cities of the First and Second Class of the Interim Committee on Cities, Kentucky General Assembly, conducted at the University of Kentucky on August 25, 1971. See *Legislative Hearing on the Future Status of Lexington*, Kentucky Legislative Research Commission, Bulletin 91 (Frankfort, 1971).

21. The plea was made by several people, including the author, at the legislative committee hearing mentioned in note 20 above. The same plea was repeated before the House Cities Committee on January 20, 1972, by the author, Mayor Foster Pettit of Lexington, and Fayette County Judge Robert Stephens.

22. The questionable features of this law were spelled out by Foster Pettit, then a candidate for mayor of Lexington, at the August 25, 1971, legislative hearing mentioned in note 20. See Bulletin 91, pp. 13–18.

CHAPTER 4

1. This much cited and widely used definition of "politics" first appeared in Harold Lasswell, *Politics: Who Gets What, When, How* (New York: New York World Publishing Co., 1958).

2. David Temple, *Merger Politics: Local Government Consolidation in Tidewater Virginia* (Charlottesville: University of Virginia Press, 1972), pp. 15–50.

3. Although this trip took place shortly after the Lexington-Fayette County Merger Commission was formally established, it was in keeping with a longstanding practice of the Lexington Chamber of Commerce to acquaint its members and friends with the advantages of city-county consolidation.

4. KRS 67A.010–.040 (1970). In 1972 the bill was amended to include counties containing second- through sixth-class cities.

5. KRS 67A.020.

6. Minutes of Governmental Options, February 1970.

7. Reeves was eliminated during the September primary, and Wallace ran fifth for a seat on the four-member city commission during the November 1969 general election.

8. Although he was ultimately acquitted of these charges, his reputation had been seriously damaged. And when it was reported that his defense attorneys from West Virginia had accepted a $25,000 city contract to investigate other alleged corrupt practices in city government, the outrage on the part of many citizens became almost impossible to contain.

9. Press release no. 1, Governmental Options, July 1970.

10. All members of the group had attended college and almost 60 percent of them had earned advanced degrees. Over a third held Ph.D. or M.D. degrees. Approximately half came from households with incomes exceeding $30,000 a year. The remaining members could be easily classified as middle to upper middle class in terms of income.

11. "The Initiators of Merger in Lexington" (Paper by Paula Feltner and Dennis Callan submitted in a graduate seminar in metropolitics at the University of Kentucky, 1973).

12. KRS 67A.020.

13. David Temple, *Merger Politics*, pp. 27–30.

14. David Booth, *Metropolitics: The Nashville Consolidation* (East Lansing: Institute for Community Development and Services, Michigan State University, 1963), pp. 16–18, 78–83. See also *Laws of Florida, 1965*, chapter 65–1502; and Schley Lyons, *Citizen Attitudes and Metropolitan Government* (Charlotte: University of North Carolina at Charlotte, 1972), pp. 8–11.

15. "City-County Government Consolidation: Columbus, Georgia," Urban Action Clearing House case study no. 18 (Washington, D.C.: Chamber of Commerce of the United States, 1971), pp. 3–4.

16. The county appointees were named on December 1, 1970. *Lexington Herald*, December 2, 1970.

17. Ibid., November 13, 1970.

18. *Lexington Leader*, January 7, 1971.

19. *Lexington Herald*, January 8, 1971.

20. The contract was officially signed February 21, 1971.

21. Resolution 28–71, City of Lexington, Kentucky.

22. According to the poll, 66 percent of all city voters interviewed said they would vote in favor of merging the city and county governments. Sixteen percent said they would vote against such a move, and 18 percent said they were not sure. "A Survey of Attitudes of Lexington Voters," conducted by John Kraft (August 1971), p. 14.

23. In addition to the unfilled seat left by the resignation of John Daughaday in the fall of 1971, the chairman of the commission received the resignations of Mrs. Frank Henry (the wife of Underwood's campaign treasurer) and Commissioner Ray Boggs, who had been defeated during the November general election. The remaining seven slots belonged to city appointees who had established a record of persistent nonattendance.

24. Similar problems confronted the proponents of city-county consolidation in Ashland-Boyd County, Kentucky. After successfully negotiating the petition requirement, the merger forces in that community met with immediate resistance. Appointments to the commission were delayed—there by a hostile county fiscal court. Little cooperation was given by county appointees. And the 1971 municipal election placed the city of Ashland in the hands of a more hostile group of political incumbents. Whereas the previous city administration reportedly had advanced a token sum of $1,500 to the merger commission, not one cent was advanced by the city and county governments after that. Thus, the Ashland-Boyd County Merger Commission was forced to rely upon the Ashland Oil Company for help, hardly a situation to allay the fears of those who view merger as a plot against ordinary citizens on the

part of dominant economic groups in the community. City-county consolidation was defeated in Ashland-Boyd County by a substantial margin in 1974.

CHAPTER 5

1. See, for example, Scott Greer, *Metropolitics: A Study of Political Culture* (New York: John Wiley and Sons, 1963), p. 191; and Schley Lyons, *Citizen Attitudes and Metropolitan Government* (Charlotte: University of North Carolina at Charlotte, 1972), pp. 53–56. Schley Lyons found that 17 percent of the voters in the Charlotte-Mecklenburg setting were unable to answer any of five simple questions about the basic features of the charter they were about to approve or disapprove at the polls. Only 13 percent were able to correctly answer more than three of the five questions.

2. Parris Glendening and John White, "Local Government Reorganization Referenda in Florida: An Acceptance and a Rejection," *Florida State University Research Bulletin* 5 (March 1968): 4.

3. The ten standing committees were as follows: government organization, representation and voting, taxation and finance, parks and recreation, public safety, transportation, housing and urban development, public health and welfare, justice, and environmental protection.

4. Bylaws of the Lexington-Fayette County Merger Commission, article 5, section 7.

5. KRS 67A.020.

6. KRS 67A.040.

7. KRS 67A.030.

8. Minutes and tape recordings of the Lexington-Fayette County Merger Commission, June 1, 1971.

9. As a member of GO, the author can testify to the fact that there was no strong consensus among the members of the group on either side of this question. The position taken by GO at the June 1, 1971, meeting had been adopted when it became known that no other group was likely to place the idea of partisan elections on the record for possible consideration.

10. The League of Women Voters, for example, had no opinion on this matter. GO suggested that it would be useful to have a fourteen-member council, eleven members to be elected from single-member districts. A spokesman for the local Chamber of Commerce thought that, whatever the size of the council, it ought to be divided equally between at-large representatives and district representatives.

11. The only direct reference to single-member district representation for municipalities in the laws and constitution of Kentucky at the time this issue was being debated by the Lexington commission was the provision allowing cities of the first through third classes with *bicameral* legislatures to employ district representation in the election of members to the more numerous "house" or "board" of the legislative body (*Kentucky Constitution,* section 160). The only other possible reference to this idea appears in the sections of the state constitution dealing with county fiscal courts. If such a court was composed of the county judge and three or more justices of the peace, it was possible to have district representation simply because justices of the peace had to be elected from districts. If, however, the court was composed of the

county judge and three county commissioners, as was the case in Fayette County and over half of all counties in the state, then the county commissions would have to reside in districts but be elected at large (*Kentucky Constitution*, sections 99, 142, 144). As long as the Lexington commission was not proposing bicameralism or a fiscal court based on the justices of the peace system as the legislative body of the new government, there was no obvious legal basis for district representation other than the premises of the Lisle argument.

12. Two members abstained, pending a decision on the type of representation system that would be employed. Minutes and tape recordings of the Lexington-Fayette County Merger Commission, June 1, 1971.

13. Ibid., July 20, 1971. See also *Lexington Leader,* July 21, 1971.

14. Minutes and tape recordings of the Lexington-Fayette County Merger Commission, July 20, 1971.

15. According to article 5, section 4 of the bylaws, a majority vote of the commission was required to pass any measure that was to be made part of the proposed charter.

16. Minutes and tape recordings of the Lexington-Fayette County Merger Commission, September 21, 1971.

17. Ibid., October 19, 1971.

18. KRS 67A.020.

19. KRS 67A.030.

20. See Vincent Marando, "Factors Affecting Voter Response to City-County Consolidation" (Paper delivered before the Conference on Integration of Metropolitan Governments, Louisiana State University at New Orleans, 1972).

CHAPTER 6

1. Minutes and tape recordings of the Lexington-Fayette County Merger Commission, January 18, 1972.

2. Ibid.

3. The spectator was Carl Penske, a local Republican who had sought several elected offices during the preceding several years. Up to this point he was the only person calling for partisan elections. As we shall see, he persisted in his cause right up to the final meeting of the commission. The recommended salary seemed large compared to the $7,200 specified in state law for mayors of second-class cities. But it reflected the desire of the commission to have a full-time mayor who would be paid a full-time salary. Furthermore, the figure of $25,000 was consistent with the salary that had to be paid a mayor of a first-class city under law.

4. The general and item veto powers of the mayor were set forth in section 5.05.

5. Section 5.08 of the proposed charter as passed by the executive committee on February 15, 1972.

6. He should have been pleased, since these provisions closely resembled the contents of an unsuccessful bill sponsored by the Kentucky City Managers' Association during the 1972 session of the state legislature. Not only

had Maroney been active in helping to promote this bill, he had called it to the attention of the local merger commission as a model for it to follow.

7. Minutes and tape recordings of the Lexington-Fayette County Merger Commission, March 21, 1972.

8. Edgar Wallace, who had run for a seat on the city commission in 1971, seemed to be thinking of running for a district council seat. And perhaps one or two others, though not so open about the subject as Wallace, seemed to be considering running for office should the charter be adopted by the voters. There were no overt pressures from incumbent officeholders. Perhaps this was because all city commissioners and all members of the Fayette County Fiscal Court were elected at large. Thus, the merger commission was not called upon to deal with anyone's particular electoral bailiwick.

9. Minutes and tape recordings of the Lexington-Fayette County Merger Commission, April 18, 1972. Several very minor technical changes were subsequently made by the commission on June 20, 1972.

10. Some students were included in District 3, but all of the very large concentrations were in District 4. Several student leaders were later to charge the commission with intentionally splitting up the student vote in the community.

11. The basic problem was that all University of Kentucky students had been counted as residents of Fayette County by the United States Census Bureau. Yet, from a purely electoral perspective, past experience suggested that an overwhelming percentage of these students maintained their voter registrations in their home states or counties.

12. The office of city assessor would be eliminated.

13. *Constitution of Kentucky,* sections 140 and 144.

14. Under article 10, the Lexington Municipal Court would be eliminated and its duties assigned to the appropriate county courts. Thus, the former county court system would become the judicial branch of the proposed merged government.

15. The Fiscal Court, according to the charter, would retain its powers to: (a) levy the ad valorem and other taxes used to support the existing consolidated public school system; (b) advise the state Department of Highways concerning what local roads ought to be maintained under the state rural highways funds; and (c) appoint one person to serve along with the county judge and the county attorney on a County Budget Commission in the event the courts held that an urban county government was, for certain state budgeting purposes, to be construed as a county government. (State law required all counties to have a budget commission to review the local county budget and submit it to the state government.)

16. This was the substance of a report given by Jerry Frock, who was then the Fayette County fiscal officer and a member of the merger commission. Minutes and tape recordings of the Lexington-Fayette County Merger Commission, April 18, 1972.

17. Neither won a seat on the new council during the general election in November of 1973.

18. The idea was to put the CAO in direct charge of a staff agency that would include divisions of personnel, budgeting, and federal programs.

19. This served to maintain the arrangement ordered by the Fayette County Fiscal Court in 1971.

20. Minutes and tape recordings of the Lexington-Fayette County Merger Commission, April 18, 1972.

21. The executive board of the Fayette County Children's Bureau was transformed into the nucleus of a new Social Services Advisory Board to advise the new Department of Social Services. The County Parks and Recreation Board was simply abolished. The city ran its parks and recreation programs under a line department and its advisory board was scheduled to be retained to serve the new Urban County Parks and Recreation Department.

22. Minutes and tape recordings of the Lexington-Fayette County Merger Commission, June 20, 1972.

23. Although the city civil service system had been abused in the past, it was the only working system in the local setting. It was therefore decided to use this as the basis of the initial classified civil service system under the new charter. A provision was added to section 9.04 to require the new government to develop a comprehensive plan for the classified civil service within two years after the new charter went into effect.

24. The charter did say that these employees would be subject to examination and certification for any further promotions or changes in their initial classification status.

25. City police and fire personnel had one pension plan and all other city civil servants had another plan.

26. Minutes and tape recordings of the Lexington-Fayette County Merger Commission, June 20, 1972.

CHAPTER 7

1. These figures exclude the separate ad valorem tax that was technically imposed by the Fayette County Fiscal Court to support the consolidated city-county school district.

2. In fiscal 1971–1972, for example, the county obtained 76 percent of its revenues from ad valorem taxes, 13.7 percent from the state, and about 12 percent from various fees. *Fayette County 1971–72 Program Budget.*

3. *Budget of the City of Lexington, 1972.*

4. Mayor Briley's remarks on this point were made in the course of praising the commission for including the idea of Partial Urban Services Districts in its proposed charter. Further details concerning the concept of "partial" districts are provided later in this chapter. *Lexington Leader,* October 12, 1972.

5. Minutes and tape recordings of the Lexington-Fayette County Merger Commission, December 21, 1971.

6. Ibid., January 18, 1972.

7. Ibid., February 15, 1972.

8. Although only twenty-four members were present that night, the staff secured the signatures of twenty-nine members prior to submitting the formal resolution to have the question of adopting the charter on the November

ballot to the Fayette County Clerk. One member was ill and could not be reached.

CHAPTER 8

1. Several hundred mimeographed copies of the proposed charter, as adopted by the Lexington-Fayette County Merger Commission on June 20, 1972, were prepared and circulated to interested persons during the three-week delay.

2. *Lexington Herald,* July 18, 1972.

3. The Fayette Circuit Court's opinion upholding KRS 67A was eventually upheld by the Kentucky Court of Appeals on August 24, 1972. See *Pinchback et al. v. Stephens et al.,* 484 SW 2d 327.

4. Observers of other merger attempts have mentioned this attitude on the part of some "civic reformers" who get involved in merger campaigns. See: David Booth, *Metropolitics: The Nashville Consolidation* (East Lansing: Michigan State University, 1963), pp. 84–85; Vincent Marando, "Factors Affecting Voter Response to City-County Consolidation" (Paper delivered before the Conference on Integration of Metropolitan Government, Louisiana State University at New Orleans, 1972), pp. 28–30; S. J. Makielski, Jr., *City-County Consolidation: A Guide for Virginians* (Charlottesville: University of Virginia, 1971), pp. 13–15; and Schley Lyons, *Citizen Attitudes and Metropolitan Government: City-County Consolidation in Charlotte* (Charlotte: University of North Carolina at Charlotte, 1972), pp. 2–4.

5. Based on observations made during the final week of the 1971 Augusta campaign when the author and Richard Engstrom were doing the research for their article entitled "Socio-Political Crosspressures and Attitudes toward Political Integration of Urban Governments," *Journal of Politics* 35 (August 1973): 682–711.

6. Walter Lippmann's phrase. See his *Public Opinion* (New York: Penguin, 1972), pp. 198–215.

7. H. H. Hyman and P. B. Sheatsley, "Some Reasons Why Information Campaigns Fail," *Public Opinion Quarterly* 11 (Fall 1947): 413–23. For a good summary of the now vast literature on political persuasion and the effects of campaigns, see Jarol Manheim, *The Politics Within* (Englewood Cliffs, N.J.: Prentice-Hall, 1975), pp. 72–110.

8. One could turn to the data concerning voter support in the few communities where referenda were held to decide whether to create the charter commission. But it is questionable whether such referenda results in Tampa, Florida (1967), Athens, Georgia (1969), or Columbus, Georgia (1970), provide an adequate measure of attitudes toward merger. See Marando, "Factors Affecting Voter Response to City-County Consolidations," pp. 6–8.

9. Schley Lyons, *Citizen Attitudes,* pp. 58–60.

10. The question was attached to the survey instrument employed by Michael Giles to gather data for his Ph.D. dissertation.

11. "A Survey of Attitudes of Lexington Voters" (unpublished report of a survey conducted in Lexington by John F. Kraft, August 1971, pp. 2–23).

12. Although support for merger has generally been higher among city

voters in other settings, it was important to discover that such a large percentage of Lexington city voters supported the idea simply because over 80 percent of all Fayette County voters lived in the city.

13. The name was stolen from the group that fought against merger in Charlotte-Mecklenburg, North Carolina, in 1971.

14. The problem of working for a Democrat was eased somewhat by the fact that the mayor of Lexington was elected on a nonpartisan ballot.

15. Some observers have estimated, for example, that each contestant in the first urban county mayoral race spent at least half again as much on his campaign.

16. For example, the Lexington Board of Realtors donated $1,000 and the local Rotary Club gave $1,500 early in the campaign.

17. Although the dining area at the Red Mile was packed on October 10, the crowd represented only a small fraction of all tickets sold. Thus many $25 tickets were sold that never cost the CIGG the price of a dinner.

18. Approximately $6,000 of CIGG funds were set aside to help pay for interviewing, coding, and computer costs.

19. Every registered voter in Fayette County was assigned a number, starting with 1. Computers were then used to generate 300 random numbers between 1 and the number of voters on the registration lists. Those voters whose assigned numbers matched those generated by the random number program fed into the computer were designated as respondents. Interviewers were required to attend training sessions before going into the field. All interviewers were paid a modest sum for their time and expenses.

20. Intensity scores for supporters and opponents were computed as follows: Strongly Support or Strongly Oppose responses were assigned 3 points; Support and Oppose responses were given 2 points; and Slightly Support or Slightly Oppose responses were given 1 point. This allowed computation of average "intensity score" for both proponents and opponents. In the 1971 poll, the average intensity score for proponents was 2.04 versus 1.40 for opponents. Using the same scoring technique in August 1972, the average intensity score for proponents and opponents was 2.30 and 2.07 respectively.

21. The RELCI index is explained in detail in Lyons and Engstrom, "Socio-Political Crosspressures," pp. 694–96. For our purposes here it is sufficient to note that respondents were given a series of five statements about how city people lived and conducted themselves. These same five items were repeated later in the interview with the term *county* substituted. Raw scores (1 through 6) for each item on the city-directed set of questions were subtracted from those given on the county-directed items. The sum of these differences, plus 25 to avoid negative numbers, provided the RELCI score for each respondent. The resulting scale ranged between zero (intense procity identifications) and 50 (intense procounty identifications). Although a score of 25 marked complete indifference, it was decided to expand the indifferent category to include scores from 23 to 27.

22. Lyons and Engstrom, "Socio-Political Crosspressures," pp. 699–711.

23. Tax-benefit orientations were measured by voter responses to a single

question about whether they thought merger would bring them "more," "fewer," or the "same" benefits for their tax dollar. A more extended discussion of this measure appears ibid., pp. 697–98.

24. The RELRT scale is fully discussed ibid., pp. 695–97. In terms of scale construction, it is similar to the RELCI index. One set of questions focused on how the local government of each respondent (i.e., city or county) operated and conducted its affairs. The other set was identical in terms of substantive content but asked the respondents how they thought the proposed merged government would operate and conduct its affairs.

25. Ibid., pp. 699–703.

26. It would mean, for example, becoming part of a totally new local government with different institutions, leaders, and traditions.

27. The proportion of blacks in the sample was slightly over 8 percent. While this is considerably below the percentage of blacks in the total population of Lexington and Fayette County, it came very close to the percentage on the voter registration lists.

CHAPTER 9

1. The goal was to have at least one coffee in each of the 116 precincts, and preferably two. There were some precincts, particularly those in which there were large numbers of apartment dwellers or large numbers of lower-income residents, where the CIGG was unable to find sponsors for a coffee. There were, however, many precincts where two coffees were scheduled.

2. Where only one coffee was held, cards were sent to all households containing a registered voter. If two or more coffees were arranged in a precinct, cards were sent to those households in the vicinity of the host. The CIGG also supplied the coffee and all necessary equipment in order to encourage people to serve as hosts.

3. *Lexington Leader,* October 31, November 1–3, and November 6, 1972.

4. Large (5½-by-8½-inch) cards were used for all mailings rather than brochures inserted into envelopes, because it is rather hard to throw a card away without glancing at it.

5. S. J. Makielski, Jr., *City-County Consolidation: A Guide for Virginians* (Charlottesville: University of Virginia, 1971), p. 175.

6. A special printing of article 9 of the proposed charter was handed out to all city and county employees so that they could read the protections built into the charter on the question of civil service and pension rights.

7. *Lexington Leader,* November 1, 1972.

8. The contents of this letter were also used in a rather large-size newspaper ad paid for by the CIGG under a large caption designed to attract the attention of farmers. It was a last-minute investment in trying to reach a group of voters that had been largely ignored in the campaign up to that point, mainly because the August 1972 survey showed that the rural voters were among the more discernible opponents of merger. This ad, it can be said, constituted the most expensive and overt effort on the part of the CIGG to convert rather than reinforce voter attitudes.

9. *Lexington Leader,* November 4, 1972. His major attacks centered on

the increased costs that he thought merger would bring and on his own preference for annexation rather than merger.

10. The antimerger movement was so trivial and so unpublicized that reporters and program chairmen for various groups called CIGG headquarters seeking information about where they might find someone to speak against merger.

11. The charter commission member was William Cundiff. He had contributed little to the preparation of the charter and had come very close to being one of those Underwood appointees who had to be replaced for nonattendance when Pettit assumed the office of mayor. But he had voted for the commission motion to recommend the adoption of the charter and signed the resolution to have the question of its adoption placed on the November ballot.

12. The 1970 United States Census had counted all students living in dormitories, apartments, or fraternity and sorority houses on or near the University of Kentucky campus as part of the total Lexington-Fayette County population. One could make the case, therefore, that substantial proportions of the population of Districts 3 and 7, as defined in the proposed charter, were UK students. But representation districts had to be based on population and not registered voters. And anyone connected with UK or local politics knew that, despite their numbers in terms of population figures, most UK students were not registered in Fayette County.

13. The promerger forces had people at each precinct handing out sample ballots showing voters where on the machine they could cast their vote for merger.

14. Vincent Marando, "Factors Affecting Voter Response to City-County Consolidation" (Paper delivered before the Conference on Integration of Metropolitan Government, Louisiana State University at New Orleans, 1972), pp. 17–18.

15. Voter turnout in Fayette County far exceeded the national level and was among the best turnouts in the state of Kentucky.

16. *Lexington Herald,* November 8, 1972.

CHAPTER 10

1. *Pinchback et al.* v. *Stephens et al.,* 484 S.W. 2d 327 (1972).

2. Holsclaw and Pinchback were also the plaintiffs in the suit that tested the constitutionality of the enabling legislation.

3. The local urban renewal agency objected to the section of the charter that sought to abolish the agency and place its functions under a line department. The Civil Service Employees Association of the city of Lexington sought to clarify the meaning of article 9 of the charter.

4. Among the ten particulars held invalid by the circuit court were the provisions that allowed the mayor to serve two consecutive terms, the section providing for per diem compensation for the first mayor and members of the first council during the interim between their election and the effective date of the charter, and the sections terminating the local urban renewal agency.

5. *Lexington Herald-Leader,* November 3, 1973.

6. *Lexington Leader,* December 28, 1973.

7. *Lexington Herald-Leader,* November 3, 1973.

8. *Holsclaw and Pinchback* v. *Stephens et al.,* 507 S.W. 2d 462 (1974).

9. Although Circuit Judge Barker had acknowledged the "unique form" argument at several points in his decision, he chose to declare the new government a form of municipal government under section 160 of the state constitution. Having done so, he had to find a way around the provisions of section 160 which seemed to allow district representation only where a municipality had a bicameral legislative body. It was a tight legal squeeze, but Barker managed to uphold district representation by declaring that the relevant portions of section 160 concerning representation flew in the face of the provisions in the state bill of rights granting citizens the right to "alter, reform or abolish their government in such manner as they may deem proper."

10. The council has since agreed to pay members of the Fiscal Court $50.00 per year.

11. Particularly troublesome were such questions as which individuals would be designated as county employees and thereby lose such benefits as pensions and civil service protections, if such a contract were revoked.

12. Section 15.04, which was held constitutional by the courts, contains the following provisions:

In the interest of planning and scheduling the full implementation of this Charter, the first Mayor and the members of the first Council of the Lexington-Fayette Urban County Government elected under the provisions of Section 15.01 above are hereby authorized and empowered to perform the following limited powers and functions during the period between their election and the effective date of this Charter:

A. Hold meetings, establish committees, and plan for the initial organization and staffing of the Urban County Government

B. Consider and nominate persons to fill the offices of Chief Administrative Officer and Commissioners of all Executive Departments in accordance with the provisions of this Charter

C. Prepare such initial budgetary and financial plans as may be necessary to govern the fiscal activities of the Urban County Government during the period between January 1, 1974 and the beginning of the first fiscal year for said government on July 1, 1974, and

D. Perform such other acts as may be necessary to the planning and scheduling of the implementation of this Charter.

13. Amato had 156 votes in the Aylesford precinct to Pettit's 73. With the precinct thrown out, Amato's overall 112-vote margin would have been cut by 83 votes, leaving him the winner by 29 votes. With the results reversed not only were the 83 votes lost to Amato, but they were added to Pettit's total, bringing it 54 votes ahead of Amato's.

14. *Lexington Leader,* December 28, 1973.

15. *Lexington Herald,* January 1, 1974.

16. Ibid., January 16, 1974.

17. Ibid., January 18, 1974.

18. Only three members of the new council had ever held public office before. And according to a survey conducted by some Georgetown (Ky.)

College students, over half had never been "very involved" in local politics or public affairs before they were elected. *Lexington Leader,* January 3, 1974.

19. One of the major tasks assigned to the new mayor and council was to prepare an initial budget for the new government. But the charter specified that the mayor was to be the chief executive and that as such he was to prepare and submit all budgets to the council. Thus, the dispute over who would be the first mayor left the new council unable to act on the interim budget mentioned in section 15.04.

20. In addition to Gulley only four other individuals were ever publicly identified with the demerger effort. One was Richard "Tiger" Cox, who had opposed merger on a local call-in radio talk show in 1972. Another was William Jacobs, a local lawyer who also had opposed merger. The third was John Goodloe, who reportedly was connected with the local American Party organization. Finally, there was Earl Wallace, Jr., whose views on merger seemed to fit neatly with those of Gulley.

21. Their efforts again attracted public attention in early July 1975. See: *Louisville Courier-Journal,* July 6, 1975; and the *Lexington Leader,* July 9, 1975.

22. *Lexington Leader,* September 3, 1975.

23. *Louisville Courier-Journal,* September 5, 1975.

Index

〜〜〜〜〜〜〜〜〜〜〜〜〜〜〜〜〜〜〜〜〜〜〜〜〜〜〜〜〜〜〜